little
footsteps

little footsteps

by Ted Tally

Nelson Doubleday, Inc.
Garden City, New York

For my own authors,
David Kenneth Tally
and Dorothy Spears Tally

Little Footsteps was first performed on February 13, 1986 at Playwrights Horizons in New York City. It was directed by Gary Pearle. The set was designed by Thomas Lynch, the costumes by Ann Hould-Ward, and the lighting by Nancy Schertler. Music was composed by John McKinney, sound effects were designed by Scott Lehrer, and the fight sequences were choreographed by B.H. Barry. The production stage manager was M.A. Howard, and the assistant stage manager was J.R. MacDonald. The Artistic Director of Playwrights Horizons is Andre Bishop.

The cast was as follows:

BEN	*Mark Blum*
JOANIE	*Anne Lange*
CHARLOTTE	*Jo Henderson*
GIL	*Thomas Toner*

The writing of this play was made possible by generous grants from the Hale Matthews Foundation and from the National Endowment for the Arts.

little
footsteps

"Fear is the third parent."
—overheard remark

CHARACTERS

BEN
JOANIE
CHARLOTTE
GIL

Ben and Joanie are in their early 30s,
Charlotte and Gil in their mid 50s.

ACT ONE

Ben and Joanie's apartment. A Sunday afternoon
in late autumn. The present.

ACT TWO

The same room. A Sunday afternoon in early spring.

ACT ONE

A nearly empty room in Ben and Joanie's apartment.

A Sunday afternoon in late autumn. The present.

We get the sense of quite an old brownstone, subdivided and renovated. High ceiling, elaborate plaster trim, wide moldings along the floor, at the top of the walls, and around the window and doors. Up center, french doors open onto the main hall. A floor-to-ceiling bookcase with track lighting is built into the facing wall of the hallway. We are at the end of this hall, but taken to stage left, it would lead to the front door, living room, and bedroom. On the wall, left, a swinging door to the kitchen, which connects offstage with the living room. On the right wall, a tall window, open partway, through which is visible a sliver of the fire escape and a wall of the neighboring building. The window's metal security gate (accordion-style, hinged to the inside of the window frame) has been left open today.

This was formerly the dining room. It has recently been repainted a bright white. The lovely old wooden floor is protected by a canvas drop cloth. The french doors, which are flung wide open, may still have their glass panes lined with masking tape. One door may even have been taken all the way off its hinges (to ease the removal of furniture); if so, it might rest on its side out in the hallway. A second drop cloth has been draped over the hallway bookcase. Scattered about are aluminum trays, brushes, cans of paint in assorted colors and sizes, cans of spray paint, cleaning rags, water buckets, etc. Some of these supplies sit in a large plastic milk crate, down left, while others are piled at right center, on the drop cloth, or upstage in the hallway. There is a second milk crate which is empty and can be moved about and used either for sitting or to stand on for better reach in painting. There is also an open stepladder, up left, to the side of the french doors; a spattered painter's smock hangs from it, and it may also have a clip-on lamp attached.

The walls are bare except for several large images, drawn or painted directly on them. These are stylized in a childlike but highly artful manner, and might include: a sleepy man-in-

3

the-moon face, stars, falling leaves, water lilies and grasses, flowers, butterflies and birds on the wing, lots of sky, and a jolly, smiling, anthropomorphic sun. Some few of these decorations appear to be already completed, but most exist only as brown paper stencils, taped in position and outlined with broad charcoal lines (where the stencils have already been removed, the outlines remain). Here and there a bit of blue sky has been painted in, or perhaps a butterfly, but the walls are still predominantly white.

The most eye-catching area of completed color represents a rainbow. This begins in a fluffy patch of stenciled clouds above the french doors, then arches left (over the position of the stepladder) before sweeping impressively down toward the floor. It is, in effect, the centerpiece of the mural's composition.

(Lights up on BEN, *down center, in front of the curtain. He wears boxer shorts, a T-shirt, socks and sneakers. He has an edgy charm, and a relentless need for just the sort of spotlight in which he now stands)*

BEN: *(To audience)* Baby joke, okay? A Catholic, a Protestant, and yes, of course, a Jew, are all asked, "What is the moment at which life begins?" And the Catholic says, "At the precise instant of conception." The Protestant says, "On the day that we're born." And the Jew says, "When the kids go off to college and the dog dies." *(Pause)* I guess that more or less sums up my own anxieties about becoming a

4

father. Not that I have a dog . . . But sooner or later, guys —sooner or later, Mother Nature sneaks up behind us, taps us on the shoulder, and delivers her sucker punch. It always goes something like this . . .

JOANIE: *(Off)* Darling?

BEN: Yes, honey?

JOANIE: *(Off)* There's something I have to tell you. (JOANIE *enters happily from the wings. A brisk manner, stubbornly upbeat. She wears a frilly maternity dress and is gigantically pregnant. The lights widen to include both* BEN *and* JOANIE) We're going to have a baby!

BEN: *(Genuine shock)* You're kidding!

JOANIE: No I'm not. It's due tomorrow.

BEN: But . . . how did this happen?

JOANIE: Well, apparently we combined strands of deoxyribonucleic acid to form a zygote. *(He stares at her blankly)* You're not disappointed, are you?

BEN: Me? Of course not! Ha ha ha, what a thought! No, I'm just a little surprised . . . is all.

JOANIE: You mean you never noticed that I stopped having my period?

BEN: *(Combing his memory)* No . . .

JOANIE: Or that my stomach was getting bigger every month, and my breasts?

BEN: I don't *think* so . . .

5

JOANIE: You didn't see I was throwing up all the time, and had heartburn and gas? *(He shakes his head)* Hemorrhoids? Constipation? Vaginal discharge?

BEN: *(To audience)* Gross me out, huh?

JOANIE: You don't recall my cramps? *(Pause)* Backaches, dizziness, swollen ankles, stretch marks . . . weird mood changes? None of those rings a bell?

BEN: I like that part about your breasts getting bigger. Will they stay that way?

(She sighs, then crosses to hug him)

JOANIE: Ben, you've been a good husband to me. You're smart, you're sweet, and you can always make me laugh. But sometimes, darling, I wonder if you're not just a little bit too wrapped up in yourself.

BEN: Hey, this feels like a balloon.

JOANIE: *(Laughs)* It's not! It's our baby.

BEN: I'm pretty sure it's a balloon. It feels squeaky.

JOANIE: Ben, I ought to know! I've carried it for thirty-nine weeks.

BEN: Then you won't mind if I just check for myself.

(He unhooks a safety pin from the waistband of his shorts, holds it up)

JOANIE: What are you—? *(Horrified)* Ben, don't you dare!

BEN: *(Grabs her arm)* Hold still.

JOANIE: Stop it! Let me go!

BEN: It'll just take a second.

JOANIE: This isn't funny! You'll hurt it! STOPPPPPP!

(She struggles for a few moments, then finally he manages to yank her closer. He pricks her dress front with the pin. There's a muffled pop, and her belly deflates. She stares at it, stunned, then looks at him)

BEN: *(Cocky)* See? Ordinary dimestore balloon. *(He closes the safety pin and tosses it away)*

JOANIE: You *bastard.* *(She moves quickly, seizing his crotch in a violent grip and then twisting)*

BEN: OWWWWWW!

(She releases him and backs away, still furious. Then abruptly she turns and runs off into the wings. He limps after her a few steps, embarrassed and in pain)

BEN: Joanie? Hey, *Joanie . . . ? (He sighs heavily, looks at us again)* She, ah . . . she didn't mean that. *(Pause)* I mean, that wasn't even the real Joanie. *(Pause)* In fact, it's such a rare event for the *real* Joanie ever to get mad, I have to more or less *imagine* what it might be like . . .

(He takes a pack of cigarettes from the back waistband of his shorts, removes a lighter and a cigarette from the pack, lights up. On this action, the curtain is rising behind him, revealing the fully lit room. We hear the sounds of distant city traffic through the partially open window—these sounds will continue, at a low level, throughout the act. He takes an appreciative puff on his cigarette, still gazing out at us)

7

My dining room, folks. *(Pause)* At least it *used* to be my dining room, before Joanie got her hands on it . . .

(He moves into the room, looking around at the wall paintings. He sets his cigarette pack down on the windowsill)

See, the thing about my wife—the reason she's such a rare person—is that she's almost incredibly *nice*. I mean just look! Oh, she hates it when people say that—says it makes her sound like some kind of wimp. But no matter how much she resents the label, she's still stuck with the quality. Joanie is "nice" the way Mozart "wrote a few tunes"—you know what I'm saying? Not a mean bone in her body. Not a molecule of spite. Joanie . . . Joanie thinks that all human disasters can be kept at bay, if only she writes enough thank-you notes.

(He kneels by the pile of paints at right center, throws a cleaning rag over his shoulder. He selects a brush, then stirs an open can of blue paint, using the stick that's sitting in the can)

But the thing is—even though she's such a good person, I can't seem to resist being mean to her. And I love her, I really do! But sometimes it's almost like I'm compelled to be this total shit, just so I can admire how well she copes with it. *(He rises, replacing the stick)* What can I tell you? I am *not* nice.

(He starts toward the ladder, carrying his can of paint, then pauses)

Oh, listen, by the way. Joanie gets really pissed if she finds out I've been smoking, so don't tell her you saw me, okay? Thanks a lot.

(He crosses, sets down his paint on the ladder's shelf, dips his brush, then starts toward the wall. He hesitates again)

8

Something else you should understand about all this. It's not that I don't like kids. Hey, I do! I'm walking in the park and I see some dad scraping bubblegum off his little girl's shoe—it just tears me up inside. You know what I mean? *(Pause)* The thing is, though—I like kids in the abstract. But when I have a kid, he won't *live* in the abstract. He'll live in my apartment. Right here. Which, let's face it, is already crammed with one husband, one wife, eight years' worth of furniture, and enough electronic *tchotchkes* to start a Crazy Eddie's. So we're not just talking about the cosmic wonder of creation here. We're dealing with a Manhattan real estate problem.

(Still puffing on his cigarette, he turns back to the wall, raises his brush to finally start painting around one of the charcoal outlines. Then he pauses yet again)

Which might be *one* reason why the very notion of—what? . . . engendering an offspring . . . has always struck me as an extremely hazy concept. Take for instance sperm. Oh sure, you *hear* a lot about them—but has anybody actually *seen* one? I mean, to me, sperm cells are like nuclear missiles. You know they *exist* . . . somewhere, lurking . . . you know they could make your life very, very unpleasant someday . . . so you just try not to think about them. And you pray to God they're never fired off with a serious intent. *(Sound of a door opening, off, and* JOANIE's *voice)*

JOANIE: *(Off)* Ben? I'm back!

BEN: Oh, Christ! *(He tosses his cigarette into the paint can, drops his brush on the ladder shelf, then hurries across the room, waving his arms to scatter the smoke. He shouts—)* You're early!

JOANIE: *(Off)* I caught the Metroliner! Where *are* you?

9

BEN: I'm in here! I just have to—I'll just be a second! *(He runs to the milk crate, down left, searching desperately among the supplies. To the audience—)* You guys keep a lid on it, okay? *(He finds a breath spray, sprays his mouth three or four times, then squirts more spray into the air around him. As* JOANIE *enters through the french doors, he hides the spray behind his back)*

JOANIE: Hi, honey! God, I missed you! *(She hurries to him happily, gives him a big hug, dropping her things—a weekend bag with a shoulder strap and a small suitcase. She wears a heavy cardigan, overalls and a tennis shirt. She is more modestly pregnant than in her first appearance —perhaps six months. He returns her hug cautiously, and after a moment she separates from him, looking down at his boxer shorts)* What are you *wearing*?

BEN: My underwear.

JOANIE: *(Looking around)* You sure haven't done much painting in here. What've you been up to?

BEN: Well . . . you know.

(He picks up her suitcase, sets it out of the way down left, near the milk crate)

JOANIE: Ben, you *promised!*

BEN: I couldn't find anything to wear! And I didn't want to mess up my good clothes.

JOANIE: What was wrong with blue jeans?

BEN: Are you kidding? I can't paint in forty-dollar designer jeans!

JOANIE: Then, wear a different pair! Those faded ones, with all the patches . . .

BEN: Those cost *sixty* dollars.

JOANIE: Ben, it's washable paint! And if Dr. Latimer says it won't hurt the baby, then how could it hurt your crummy old pants? *(She looks around, annoyed)* God, we're so far *behind* now . . . *(Pause. Then, more cheerfully)* Well, never mind . . . we'll do it together. *(She kisses him. He turns his face, taking the kiss on his cheek)* That'll be more fun anyway! *(She exits through the french doors, grabbing up her weekend bag)*

BEN: *(Mutters as she goes)* Goody-goody . . .

JOANIE: *(Off)* What?

BEN: Nothing! *(He tosses the breath spray back into the milk crate, then sits on her suitcase)* How are your folks? . . . Mom okay? Dad, too?

JOANIE: *(Off)* They're fine. You know . . . For them.

BEN: That's good. Did they miss me?

JOANIE: *(Reentering)* Well, if they did, they managed to conceal their grief.

BEN: Aren't they sweet.

(She is carrying a large sketchbook, scissors, and several folded stencils. She sets these down on the floor, then takes off her cardigan and drapes it over the cross-brace of the ladder. Her painter's smock is hanging there, and she takes a bandanna from its pocket)

11

JOANIE: We had a *classic* last night at dinner. Mom was going on and on, in that subtle way she has, about this big fancy-pants christening they'd just been to at Trinity Episcopalian. White silk gown, silver rattle, the whole nine yards. *(She twirls the bandanna into a tight strap, then brushes her hair off her forehead and ties it down)* And I said to her, "You know, Mom, if this baby is a boy, Ben's parents are going to expect us to have a *bris* instead." And she actually said to me—are you ready—?

BEN: Oh, you're *kidding.*

JOANIE: I swear to God. "What's a *bris?*"

BEN: You didn't *tell* them, did you?

JOANIE: Sure I did! *(She kneels by her sketchbook, picks up a large stencil—a butterfly—and begins cutting out the folded shape)*

BEN: Joanie . . . your parents still think of "Jews" as Old Testament camel-jockeys. If you go spilling the beans about our savage rituals, you'll just confirm their prejudice.

JOANIE: My parents are not prejudiced! They're . . . sheltered. You don't meet a lot of Jews in Chadd's Ford.

(BEN suddenly spots the cigarette pack, sitting in plain view on the windowsill)

BEN: *(Under his breath)* Damn!

JOANIE: What is it? Something wrong?

BEN: No, no—just—thinking about your parents . . . *(He rises, edges between her and the window as casually as possible)*

12

JOANIE: Anyway—what *are* we going to do about it?

BEN: What are we going to do about what? *(He begins to ease himself backward, toward the window)*

JOANIE: The service. The naming. You know—religion.

BEN: *(Shrugs)* Same as everybody else, I guess. Lapsed humanism?

JOANIE: *(A bit sadly)* We never talk about stuff like that. You know? I mean, how is it we could've known each other almost eight years, and yet we never had this conversation before?

BEN: We were never pregnant before.

JOANIE: I'm serious, Ben! Is this kid going to be Jewish, or Episcopalian, or what?

BEN: Maybe we could somehow . . . *combine* the two services. You know—call it a "bristening." *(He laughs, rather too heartily. He has reached the window and is leaning against the sill. He fumbles behind himself, reaching blindly for the cigarette pack. She stares at him)*

JOANIE: What've you got in your hands?

BEN: Mmm? *(Pause, then surprise)* Oh, *these!* (Brings out cigarettes) I found them.

JOANIE: *(Wearily)* Mmm-hmm.

BEN: Must've been left here by one of the workmen. I was just throwing them away—look—

JOANIE: *(Sighs)* Could I see them for a moment, please?

13

BEN: Sure! No problem. *(He crosses meekly and allows her to snatch away the pack)*

JOANIE: I'm tired of this argument, Ben. I'm not going to have it again.

BEN: I found them! I was throwing them away!

JOANIE: Fine. I believe you.

BEN: *(Crossing away)* I did! They were right here! Right over here is where I found them . . .

(She rips the pack open, tosses the lighter aside, dumps the cigarettes into her hands, and shreds them violently. When she's finished, she dusts her hands off onto the floor)

JOANIE: *(On her action)* I *said* I believe you. But if you won't think of your own health, and you don't care about mine, then I wish you'd at least think about the baby.

BEN: Oh, yeah. *Him* again . . .

JOANIE: Or her. *(She goes to him impulsively, takes him by the wrists)* Feel. Put your hands right here.

BEN: Aw, I've got paint all over—

JOANIE: Never *mind!* Just feel . . . *(She places his palms flat against her belly, holds them there. A long silence while they look at one another. He feels her gently, looks down at her bulk)*

BEN: *(Quietly, with wonder)* It's so solid. So *dense.* Not at all like . . .

JOANIE: Like what?

14

BEN: *(Pause)* Nothing.

JOANIE: That's us, Ben. A part of *us*. Don't you know that whatever *I* eat, *she* eats? And whatever I breathe, she breathes too?

BEN: Or he does.

JOANIE: Or he does. *(Pause)* Do you want him to be born with stunted lungs?

BEN: Hell, no. Let him work for them, like I had to. *(She pulls away from him impatiently, but he catches her by the waist, holds her close. He kneels, putting his ear against her belly)* He's running another marathon. Can you tell?

JOANIE: Don't try to change the subject.

BEN: Go, kid, go! There's the finish line—just one guy left to beat! *(He glances up at JOANIE, grins)* "Fetus, don't fail me now!"

JOANIE: I'm still mad at you, Ben. *(But she can't help being amused. Partly to hide this, she kneels again at her sketch pad and resumes cutting the stencil. He rises, circles her)*

BEN: What's it *like* in there? What sort of *day* do you have? I've been wondering about that a lot lately, trying to see if any of it might come back to me . . . I mean, for one thing, we know it's *cramped*.

JOANIE: Not to her, it's not. You're just projecting.

BEN: It's *hot* as hell too, and you've got all this water goosh- ing around. Gooosh . . . gooooossshhh! *(He kneels behind her, pushing against her playfully, trying to distract her from her work)* It must feel like you're wearing a Jacuzzi! And the *light* is weird, I think, it's all . . . blood-red and translucent. *(Pause)* So I'm floating in here . . . sort of snorkeling . . . and I've got these spooky *sounds* coming at me . . . like echoes maybe. And I can't get away from them! I'm trapped! Ba-da-BOOM! What was *that?* Ba-da-BOOM! It's Mama's heartbeat, right in my ear! (JOANIE *smiles)* And—what's that *other* weird noise? *(Softly)* Rumblerumblerumble . . . Sounds like it's coming from her tummy . . . rumblerumblerumbleRUMBLERUMBLE! . . . Oh, my God, I just remembered! *(Clutching her)* We drank some BEER today! Mama—she's gonna—she's gonna *burp!* RUN FOR YOUR LIVES! BURRRRRRRRR-RUP! WHOOOOOOOSSH! BA-DA-BOOM!! *(This last is right in her ear.* JOANIE *falls over, wincing, laughing outright. He half-collapses on top of her, laughing too)* No *wonder* we're so cranky when we finally get out of there! We've just spent nine months in the Twilight Zone. *(A muffled shout, into her belly)* Don't come out! This is a warning! It's weird out here, too!

JOANIE: *(Laughing)* You'll catch cold, dressed that way. And I need your help out here. *(Pushes him away)* Go put on some more clothes!

BEN: *(A bit irritated)* You're not my mother too, you know.

JOANIE: Except when it suits you.

BEN: *Ooooo!* Tsssss! *(He wets his forefinger and makes a stroke in the air, indicating to the audience a point scored for* JOANIE*)*

JOANIE: Get *out* of here! I mean it! *(She rises, props her sketchbook out of the way against a wall, to one side of the french doors)*

BEN: I'm *going*, okay? *(He exits through the french doors, but after only a moment sticks his head back in. To the audience)* Don't believe a word she says.

JOANIE: GO!!

(He exits, grinning. She shakes her head, exasperated)

Ben! Ben, Ben, BEN . . . !

(She takes her smock from the ladder. As she puts it on, she glances at the audience)

Our friends ask me why I want another baby when I've already got one. *(Pause)* Somehow that used to sound funnier . . .

(She crosses to the milk crate, down left, carrying the scissors and the cutout butterfly stencil. She drops the scissors into the crate and pulls pieces of masking tape from the edge of the crate, attaching them to the stencil)

What's he been *doing* in here, anyway—just yakking at you guys . . . ? Mmm, that's what I thought. Yakking and daydreaming. And smoking! He promised me he'd spend the whole weekend painting the sky. But, as you can see . . . Mr. Responsibility.

(She crosses to the wall, up right, where a butterfly has already been painted in pale green. She tapes up her stencil, which exactly overlaps the painted butterfly. The stencil has four holes cut in it, two on each wing)

The irony is, he's gonna make a great father. He really is! He just doesn't know it yet. And that's kind of sad, I think. He's got so much love to offer. So much energy, and imagination . . . I wish you could see him with other people's kids. At parties and stuff . . . He'll get down on the floor and hold this serious, top-secret, totally involved conversation with some two-year-old—I mean for hours! The level of camaraderie is just . . . But, then, if you ask him what

on earth they could possibly find to talk about for all that
time, he says something like, "Know your enemy."

*(She takes a plastic painting mask from her smock pocket,
pulls its cord down over her head, letting the mask rest under
her chin. Then she picks up two cans of spray paint from the
floor near the corner, up right)*

He can't fool me, though . . . I think one of Ben's greatest
gifts is that he still has so much of the kid in himself. And I
mean that in the best sense. It's one of the things I've
always loved about him.

*(With her mask pulled on, she shakes the cans of spray paint
and fills in the wing holes of the butterfly—first the broad
areas in pink, then some accenting in white. Then, after
letting the air clear for a moment, she carefully peels off the
stencil. She steps back for a better look, removing her mask.
The effect—the butterfly now has brightly colored spots—is
quite magical)*

What do you think? Too Disney? *(Pause)* I don't know, I
kind of like it . . .

*(She folds the stencil, crossing left to set it aside in the milk
crate, along with the two spray cans)*

Ben was holding out for a circus motif in here. You know—
acrobats, clowns. He wanted to surround that doorway
with tongues of flame, like it was a big hoop, and then have
a lion jumping through it. But I said, "Ben, in that case he'd
have to jump *over* the hoop, not through it." Then he got
all huffy and said I was denying his "creative input."

*(She takes BEN's can of blue paint from the ladder shelf and
crosses with it to right center, to the pile of other cans)*

Creativity is a sore spot with Ben. He works in television.

(She kneels to stir the paint. A slight pause)

Why can't he . . . why can't he just be a little bit *happier* about this? Or at least pretend he is. That's what hurts sometimes . . . I mean, all *I* have to do is walk down the street these days—or more like, roll down the street—and I get this goofy *smile* on my face. You know what I'm saying? I can't even help myself. I look at a tree and think, God!— what would *that* look like, the first time you ever saw one? Would it look like it was growing down from the sky, instead of up? What would a butterfly look like, or a rainbow, if you didn't even know they had names yet? . . . I know that sounds corny, but—can't Ben see that something is *happening* here? Something—finally!—*important* in our lives. Can't he see that all of our running around these last few years, all the *possessions* we've grabbed at so frantically, all the little so-called *achieve*ments—can't he understand yet that next to this they were *nothing?*

(Pause. She pours some paint into an aluminum tray, picks up a pair of brushes)

I know he loves me. And maybe he's even trying his best. But sometimes I just have to get *away* from him for a while, and go where I'm still allowed to feel *good* about this. You know . . . ? *(She rises)* Any*where.*

(She starts toward the wall, left, then hesitates, looking at it. She looks back to the audience)

Because to me . . . to me a rainbow still looks just a little bit like a bridge. A wonderful bridge to someplace I've never been, but always wanted to visit . . . *(Pause)* Why can't he see that too?

(BEN *reenters through the kitchen door, now wearing ratty jeans and a corduroy shirt over a T-shirt. He is finishing a sandwich, and also sipping a beer)*

19

BEN: *(To audience)* Lies, lies, a tissue of lies . . . What? What is it?

JOANIE: I guess you'd have to know sooner or later, Ben. I told them . . . you were in TV.

BEN: *(Horrified)* Oh, God, no. You didn't.

JOANIE: Sorry. Your secret is out.

BEN: *(Kneels)* Friends, I was young, I was a fool. They said I'd meet Miss Piggy.

JOANIE: Usually, to avoid embarrassment, we just pretend he's in some other occupation.

BEN: We tell people I'm a mortician, or a detective for the IRS. *(To* JOANIE, *as he rises)* Where do you need me?

JOANIE: Take down the other stencils.

BEN: Check. *(He sets down his beer and sandwich on the windowsill, then climbs the ladder to start pulling down those stencils which have already been outlined. She has begun painting blue sky on the wall, up left, using a large brush for broad areas and a smaller brush for detailed work around the stenciled or outlined forms)*

JOANIE: Actually, Ben is in television *sports.*

BEN: Actually, I'm in television sports *promotion.*

JOANIE: It's a network staff job. *(Pause)* You better explain.

BEN: Okay, it's simple. You know those shows where guys race each other around a golf course, carrying refrigerators on their backs? And starlets in wet T-shirts act as cheer-leaders?

JOANIE: In the business, they're called "trashsports."

BEN: Please, darling. "Innovative special programming."

JOANIE: Sorry, love.

BEN: Okay, well that's *not* what I do. *(He climbs down from the ladder, crosses right to pull more stencils from the far walls)*

JOANIE: *But*—you know the commercials that *tell* you about those shows?

BEN: Those little teasers that warn you not to miss next Saturday's flaming tapioca plunge? Or whatever the hell it is . . .

JOANIE: They're called "promos."

BEN: Well, *that's* what I do. I design those promos.

JOANIE: He's very good at it too.

BEN: You're damned right I am. For ten seconds a week I'm a *genius.*

JOANIE: He was a finalist for a Clio Award.

BEN: I lost out to some ex-jock doing a public-service spot on drug abuse. Depressed me so much I got stoned for a week.

JOANIE: *(Irritated)* Why do you *tell* them things like that? You know that's not true.

BEN: Okay. Two days. *(He crosses to dump his handful of stencils by the pile of paint cans at right center)*

JOANIE: Oh, you're so full of it, Ben.

21

BEN: Joanie's a little paranoid about drugs. She's afraid we did so many of them in college—

JOANIE: *You* did so many!

BEN: —*I* did so many of them, that the baby will be born looking like Flipper. (*A brief but vivid impression*) "Ork! Ork! Ork! Ork!"

JOANIE: (*Shocked*) That's not funny! Don't even *think* that!

BEN: But, honey, John Lennon's kids turned out great! And just look at Moon Unit Zappa.

JOANIE: (*Furious*) You go too far sometimes, you know that? You think you're *so* God-damned hilarious—

BEN: Hey, hey, *language*, huh?

JOANIE: —so God-damned *hip* all the time, with your little digs and your one-liners—

BEN: Honey, I've just been telling these folks how *nice* you are.

JOANIE: —telling your stupid little dead-baby jokes when our friends come over—

BEN: (*To audience*) I've *never* done that!

JOANIE: Oh, uh-huh! (*Crossing down toward audience*) "How do you make a dead baby float? One scoop of ice cream, and one scoop of dead baby."

BEN: We'll talk about this later, okay?

JOANIE: No! *No*, God damn it! We'll talk about it *now!* Because how do you think it makes *me* feel when you say things like that? Don't you think I lie awake at night—don't you know I have *nightmares* about something like that? And what if something *did* happen? You think it's so funny to joke about now, but what if it *did?* I know you, you'd freak out! You wouldn't be able to handle it! You'd be out the door like a shot, and leave me stuck with—leave m-me ss-stuck with—*(She starts to cry, turns her back angrily. She tries to start painting again)*

BEN: Ho boy . . . *(Pause. He goes to her)* Honey, that's just not—

JOANIE: Don't call me honey! *(She breaks away from him again, crossing right to the pile of cans and kneeling to get more paint)*

BEN: *(Following)* That's just not true! First of all, it's not going to happen. Okay? And second of all, we're in this thing together—one hundred percent. My God, don't you know that I would never, *ever* desert you because of something bad happening? Even though it's not *going* to happen. *(Touching her shoulders)* Don't you *know* that by now, sweetheart?

JOANIE: *(Rising, shaking free)* Don't call me sweetheart, either! You only say those things when you're mad at me.

BEN: I'm *trying* to reassure you, God damn it!

JOANIE: *(Shouting)* Well, just leave me the hell alone!

BEN: "Ork! Ork! Ork!"

(Very upset, she pulls her mask over her face and crosses back to the wall, left, to continue painting. She crouches there, near the upstage corner, with her back to the audience, pointedly ignoring BEN. He looks at the audience helplessly)

There I go again! *(Crossing down center)* What is *wrong* with me? I don't *want* to hurt her—I don't *mean* to hurt her—and I hurt her. *(Pause)* Okay, but she's overreacting, too. She really is! And this kind of—what do they call it?— "desertion anxiety"—I mean, this is absolutely *classic*. Brazelton talks about this, Caplan, Auerbach in *The Whole Child*. Even Spock! I'm not taking the rap for *all* of this . . .

(The lights have begun to dim, taking on the greenish, spooky tones of a horror film. Outside the window it becomes quite dark. BEN *is gradually isolated in a pool of light)*

The thing I have to keep telling myself is that I shouldn't *blame* Joanie for overreacting. Her hormones are playing pinball with her emotions—you know what I mean? The pregnant female—and I'm not being sexist here, okay?— the pregnant female is just not as *rational* as the male. Pure and simple.

(A sudden, very loud clap of thunder. BEN *starts in surprise. A flash of lightning at the window. The noise of street traffic has disappeared)*

God, though! *(Pause)* What if Joanie was right? *(Pause)* What if one of those jokes *did* come true? What if something went wrong with the baby? Would I be able to handle it, or would I panic like she said . . . ?

(Another clap of thunder, more lightning)

I'd probably be able to handle it. *(Pause)* I'm *sure* I'd be able to handle it . . .

*(*JOANIE *rises, turns around ominously. She has put aside her brush and buttoned her smock. She wears green plastic gloves and stares at* BEN *over the top of her painting mask. She moves forward into his circle of light)*

JOANIE: Benjamin?

BEN: *(Turns, sees her)* Oh, hiya, Dr. Latimer! Did everything come out okay in the delivery room? *(She is silent. He chuckles nervously)* That's a joke! You know—"baby?"—"come out?"

JOANIE: My poor dear Benjamin . . .

BEN: *(Growing alarmed)* It's Joanie, isn't it? Something's happened to Joanie!

JOANIE: *(Pulls mask down sadly)* Your wife is fine. I have her under sedation. She—doesn't know yet.

BEN: Know what? *(Pause)* You mean—the baby? *(She nods)* You mean it's . . . ?

JOANIE: Oh no, no, it's alive! *(Pause)* That is, we definitely *feel* that it's living.

BEN: Why—why do you say "it?" Is it a boy or a girl?

JOANIE: *(Hesitates)* Yes!

BEN: Answer me, Doctor, please!

JOANIE: Look, why split hairs? I *told* you it was alive.

BEN: *(Shaking her)* WHAT—IS—WRONG—WITH—MY—CHILD?!

JOANIE: *(Frees herself gently)* Ben, I'm going to level with you. We in the medical profession don't hit a home run every time we step up to the plate. In fact, once in a while we miss the bunt sign, and the go-ahead runner gets caught in a suicide squeeze. Ben, what I'm trying to say is, your—well, let's call him your *son*—was born without a body.

BEN: Without a *body?* Oh my God, that's horrible!

JOANIE: *(Sighs)* Yes. Yes, it is. I can only suspect that you or Joanie must have experimented at some point with a marijuana cigarette.

(She peels off her gloves and mask, stuffing them into a pocket of her smock. BEN *sits weakly on a nearby paint can)*

BEN: You mean . . . my boy is nothing but a *head?* That's all there is to him? *(She is silent)* Well, look, that's not—that's not the end of the world, is it? I mean, football is out, sure, but I can still teach him to play chess . . .

JOANIE: I only wish it were that simple, Ben.

BEN: There's more?

JOANIE: Less! Your son doesn't even have a head. In fact, he's just an eyeball. I have him right here.

(Another crash of thunder as JOANIE *takes a glass eyeball out of her pocket. As* BEN *rises, she hands it to him)*

BEN: *(Stunned)* This is . . . my son?

JOANIE: Careful how you hold him. He blinks.

BEN: My son is . . . an eyeball?

JOANIE: *(Cheerfully)* Well, yes—but rather a big one for his age.

BEN: *(Suddenly shrieking)* OH MY GOD, DOCTOR! MY SON IS AN EYEBALL! OH MY GOD! WHAT COULD BE WORSE THAN *THIS?!*

JOANIE: *(Whispers)* He's blind!

(BEN *screams, tossing the eyeball high into the air. Another crash of thunder, and more lightning.* JOANIE *catches the eye. Laughing insanely, she plops it into an open can of paint as she returns to her former position, kneeling at the up left corner.*

As the lights bump back to full, BEN *clutches his chest and gasps for breath.* JOANIE, *instantly back in character, turns from her painting, looks at him curiously. Outside, the traffic sounds have returned)*

JOANIE: Ben . . . ? What's the matter?

BEN: *(Squeaks)* Heart attack!

JOANIE: Are you serious?

BEN: This is it!

(She rushes to him, but he avoids her and begins jogging frantically in place, turning in little circles)

JOANIE: What are you *doing?* Hold still!

BEN: I can't! I've gotta keep moving!

JOANIE: I'm trying to help!

BEN: If I stop I'll die! But if I just keep jogging! Then maybe I'll feel like it's just beating fast! Because I'm jogging! And not because I'm having! A heart attack!

JOANIE: *(Holding him)* Men your age don't have heart attacks!

27

BEN: Martin Sheen did! In the jungle! When they were film-ing! *Apocalypse Now!*

JOANIE: Well, this isn't the jungle, and there's nothing wrong with your heart! Now will you just hold *still* for a second?

(She finally stops his jogging. He stares at her, panting)

You're having an *anxiety* attack! You've had them before, so we both know there's nothing to be afraid of. In a few minutes it'll go away, if you just don't panic. Okay?

BEN: *(Choking sounds)* Nnngghh—kkhh—nngghhh . . .

JOANIE: *Now* what?

BEN: *(Doubling over)* I can't breathe!

JOANIE: Then lie down.

BEN: Help me, Joanie—I can't breathe!

JOANIE: You're hyperventilating.

BEN: My left arm! It's gone numb!

JOANIE: Lie down on the floor!

BEN: *(Slapping his arm)* Just like in a heart attack!

(She trips him down onto his back, then straddles him and sits on his stomach, maneuvering her bulk awkwardly. She pins his shoulders as he writhes desperately. Offstage, their doorbell rings. JOANIE looks up in irritation, shouts)

JOANIE: We're all right, Mrs. Belnap! Go away! *(To BEN)* Stop *struggling!*

BEN: I can't! I can't hold still!

JOANIE: I mean it, Ben!

BEN: No—please—let me go! You're killing me!

JOANIE: WILL YOU SHUT THE HELL UP?!

(He stops babbling, but continues to moan softly. The door-bell rings again. JOANIE *shouts toward the hallway)*

GET LOST, YOU OLD SNOOP!!

(There is no third ring. She looks down at BEN, *who is still struggling feebly)*

Open your eyes! Open them! Focus on me! We're gonna pretend we're in Lamaze class, okay? I want you to take a long, deep breath. Listen to me! When *I* breathe, *you* breathe, okay? *(He nods)* Are you ready? Breathe . . . *innn.* Slow and steady . . . that's it, keep going . . . Good, now *hold* it for a minute. *(Pause)* Okay, now let that air out, but slowwwly . . . get every last bit of it . . . Good. Now let's just keep taking one breath at a time. Try not to think about anything else for a while. Ready, and— *innn* . . . hold it . . . and *ouuut.* Innnn . . . and hold . . . and ouuut. *Slowwwwly!*

(For a while they continue breathing in unison. JOANIE *rocks gently on his body.* BEN *stares straight up, gradually growing calmer.* JOANIE *turns to the audience)*

The first time this happened, we were in an Indian restaurant. And I'm ashamed to admit it, but—I actually laughed at him. I thought it was something to do with his chicken *vindaloo*—that he'd got it too hot or something. . . . Until he began actually *gasping* and turning blue. Then everybody got all excited and tried to give him the Heimlich maneuver. Four or five men all at once, arguing about who had the best technique. Luckily one of the waiters was pre-med . . . Later I realized it must've been some sort of delayed reaction to the baby. At that point we'd only been sure I was pregnant for three days.

BEN: *I* still think it was the chicken.

JOANIE: Keep breathing! *(Pause)* He's got this—I don't know, this obsession, almost—that he's going to die before the baby is born. Like God tries to keep an even score? Elizabeth—my therapist—says it's not uncommon.

BEN: *(Scornfully)* Oh, great, *Elizabeth. (To audience)* She's totally exaggerating.

JOANIE: Just breathe!

BEN: It's not like that at all!

JOANIE: No? Well, what triggered it *this* time?

BEN: *(Pause)* I shouldn't have said what I said about Flipper. I'm sorry.

JOANIE: I think you're dangerously insane.

BEN: I love you too, Joanie. I really and truly do. *(Pause)* But can I just say something?

JOANIE: What?

BEN: You're killing my nuts.

JOANIE: *(Sourly)* You can stop breathing now.

(She gets off him carefully, stretches her aching back muscles, then crosses to open the window wider. The traffic noise

increases slightly. BEN *remains flat on his back, staring up. A long pause)*

BEN: The workmen did a good job on the ceiling. *(Pause)* I like it down here. It's very . . . stable.

JOANIE: Feel better now?

BEN: Much better. Thanks.

JOANIE: You scared the hell out of me.

BEN: Sometimes it all just . . .

JOANIE: Just what?

BEN: *(Turning on his side)* Nothing.

(She looks at him for a long moment, sighs. She looks at the walls, then back at BEN)

JOANIE: Is this what you call painting, Ben?

BEN: I'm working myself into the mood. I'm letting these walls speak to me.

JOANIE: Do the sun. *(She crosses back to the wall, left, picks up her tray and begins painting areas of sky again)*

BEN: The sun! Riiiight! Jolly ol' smiling face of the jolly ol' sun . . . *(Pause)* What color?

JOANIE: Well, what color do you *think?*

BEN: *(Shrugs)* Depends on how much air pollution.

JOANIE: Try yellow.

BEN: Yellow! Now, there's an idea! See, Joanie *knows* about stuff like that, 'cause she's got a B.A. in art. *(He crawls about in search of yellow paint)*

JOANIE: Yeah, that plus a token will take you to SoHo.

BEN: Darling, please! *(To audience)* Captains of industry tremble at her approach.

JOANIE: You know the great thing about being an artist? It's that you get to experience so many other professions. I've worked as a secretary, shop clerk, mother's helper—

BEN: Mmmm! *That* one gave her ideas . . . *(He locates a can and begins prying off the lid with a screwdriver. It proves to be rather firmly stuck)*

JOANIE: Layout assistant for an ad agency . . . assistant scene painter for TV commercials . . .

BEN: *I* helped with that one.

JOANIE: —Which Ben helped me get, thank you, dear, but which pretty soon started to feel a little too much like *real* painting, and besides, I never would've gotten into the union, anyway.

BEN: *(Quietly)* You would have, too. You were just scared of the exam.

JOANIE: I was not!

BEN: Scared you might finally make some money, then. *(She gives him a look)* Joke! It's a joke . . . c'mon!

JOANIE: Right now I'm a volunteer assistant at the Met.

BEN: Museum, not Opera. *(With a grunt, he finally gets the lid off the can. It's the wrong color)* Damn. This is blue. *(He replaces the lid, sets the can aside)*

JOANIE: They've been very understanding about the pregnancy, and they said this winter, if I want, I can even do some tour-group lectures. *(Pause)* They *like* me there, they really do.

(BEN crosses upstage, toward the hallway, where more paint cans are piled)

BEN: "A little gal with your talents, my goodness, we're just going to have to put you on *salary* one of these days."

JOANIE: *(Pauses in her work)* You've made your point, okay?

BEN: Okay.

JOANIE: So just drop it.

BEN: My lips are sealed. *(He searches among the hallway cans)*

JOANIE: *(To audience)* All the other volunteers wear monogrammed crewnecks and have nicknames like "Sudsy." But at least I get to be *near* some art. Even if I'm not making any.

BEN: You're making some now. Right here. *(Holding up paint cans)* Hey, y'know, we're gonna look pretty silly if this turns out to be a girl.

JOANIE: What do you mean?

BEN: All this blue paint.

33

JOANIE: But we need it for the sky. You can't have the sky be *pink. (Pause)* Anyway, that's nonsense, all that stuff. Gender stereotyping. I thought we agreed.

BEN: Oh right, right . . .

(He crosses to the window with a small can of yellow paint. He retrieves his beer can, sips from it)

Where do we stand on Barbie dolls—things like that?

JOANIE: That's different.

BEN: Oh.

JOANIE: Barbie is sacred. I can't even *imagine* growing up without her.

(BEN puts aside his beer, then sits to pry open the paint can)

BEN: Maybe . . . if we have a boy, we should get *him* a Barbie. And if it's a girl, give her a Ken doll. Stamp out sexism right there in the cradle.

JOANIE: Aha! But how do you explain to them that the *Ken* doll may also have certain . . . feelings . . . toward G.I. Joe?

BEN: *Vay is mir!* Good one . . . Fifty points.

JOANIE: Ben and I play this game we call "Tough Questions." You know—sort of a rehearsal. Like, "Daddy, Daddy, why is there death?"

BEN: Or "Mommy, Mommy, what is my thing for?"

JOANIE: Or "How come God makes bag ladies?"

34

BEN: Or "Who was Leona Helmsley?"

JOANIE: *(Laughs)* All the real biggies we might have to face someday. Okay, Dad, for fifty points! I come home from school one day, I'm crying buckets—make believe I'm crying—

BEN: Buckets, right—

JOANIE: I'm fifteen years old, I'm in*cred*ibly upset. And I say to you, "Daddy, Daddy, I think I'm gay." And *you* say—?

BEN: Ah! *(Pause)* Mmm-*hmm. (Pause)* "I don't suppose there's any chance you mean 'convivial'?"

JOANIE: *"Dad-*dy! Be *serious!"*

BEN: Right. Sorry. *(Pause)* Umm . . . "Have a seat, my child." *(He motions for* JOANIE *to sit on one of the paint cans at right center. She is a bit reluctant to stop working, but sits as directed, setting her tray down beside her. He looks at her, smiles, gets no response. Then he tries a fatherly little punch on her shoulder)* "Son, listen to me—"

JOANIE: Daughter.

BEN: *Daughter?* No fair!

JOANIE: *(Firmly)* Daughter, fifteen. Sobbing.

BEN: Why do I always get the worst ones? *(She wails)* Okay, okay! (Pause. He paces awkwardly, searching for words. JOANIE *smiles at us, enjoying the game)* "Sweetheart, look —your mother and I—ah, understand what you're going through. Believe me—nobody knows better than *we* do just how scary and confusing sex can be." (JOANIE *smacks his leg. He grins)* "But hey, this isn't the Dark Ages! After all, we're in the year—" *(Pause)* What year is it?

35

JOANIE: Well, if I'm fifteen, that would make it . . .

BEN: Christ. 2001.

(Slight pause. They look at each other unhappily)

"After all, sweetheart, this is the twenty-first century! And
we just want you to know . . . to know that no matter
what choice you may ultimately make as to your, umm,
sexual preference—to know that you'll still be our child
. . . and your mother and I will still love you very, very
much." *(Pause)* How's that?

JOANIE: Not bad! But what would you *really* say?

BEN: *(Shouts)* "Homo! Homo! Homo!"

*(She jumps up, stabbing at him with her paintbrush. He
backs away, both of them laughing as he catches the wet
blows with his palms. Abruptly he clutches his chest, as if
having another of his "heart attacks." When she steps toward
him anxiously, lowering her paintbrush, he catches her off
guard and sweeps her into a hug. They kiss. It is a long
embrace, of growing intensity. Finally she becomes self-conscious about the audience. Despite his resistance, she gently
but firmly breaks off the kiss. They stand looking out at the
audience for a moment, still hugging. Pause. BEN looks at
JOANIE)*

Parenthood, huh? . . . The Unprepared attempting the
Impossible for the sake of the Ungrateful.

JOANIE: *(Smiles)* Still, though . . .

BEN: *(Sighs)* Still . . . Whatcha gonna do?

*(She separates from him, crossing to pick up her tray of
paint)*

JOANIE: It's just that people who deliberately choose *never* to have babies seem a little . . . I don't know . . . what's the word?

BEN: Happy? Peaceful? Free?

JOANIE: *(A pause, considering)* Stingy.

BEN: Stingy . . .

(She dips her brush in the tray, crosses to the corner, up right, to work on a new section of wall. He watches her for a moment, then crosses to the water bucket, amid the pile of cans at right center. He kneels to wash the paint off his hands, drying them on a rag)

You know, this morning . . . when I was up in the closet, rooting around for that towel . . . I kept coming across all this junk from college. Textbooks . . . three-ring binders . . . papers I wrote. "James Joyce: Nearsighted Visionary." Even one of my old track jerseys, all stiff with crud. I mean, just the most incredibly *useless* collection of stuff you ever saw. And I thought, why the hell did I *save* this mess all these years? I've never looked at it, not even *once*. Unless —it was to show it to my kid someday . . .

JOANIE: *(Pause)* Ben . . . that's so sweet.

BEN: Isn't it? *(Becoming self-conscious, he glances around. He sees her sketchbook, propped against the wall by the french doors. He crosses to pick it up)* Hey, did you show them these sketches yet?

JOANIE: Oh, they don't want to see those. And I wish you'd help me!

BEN: Sure they do! Are you kidding? These're fantastic! *(He flips through the pages)* They're studies for all the different wall paintings. See? Preliminary sketches. Joanie's put *weeks* into this.

JOANIE: They're really not so great. Ben, help me!

BEN: Honey, c'mon! *(Stands, holding the book higher)* This one . . . let's see . . . this one right here is the "Before" picture. Shows what this room used to look like when it was still our dining room. *(Pause)* God, the *meals* we ate in here! *(He moves about the room, remembering)* Mostly takeout, I admit, but still . . . And the parties! Birthdays, anniversaries, Christmas . . . Passover . . . *(Pause)* Lots of nice times, huh, Joanie?

JOANIE: Ben—people can still have parties even *after* they become parents. It's a new law they passed.

BEN: Oh sure, I know. *(Pause)* Remember—*(Laughs)*—remember the time we had that sit-down dinner in here for —what was it—*eighteen?*

JOANIE: *(Laughs)* Oh, Lord! And I hired that *deranged* Italian man, and made everybody wear black tie.

BEN: It was the night I lost that dumb award. Boy, did you save me then . . . *(Pause)* Anyway—I guess that's all just . . . watercress under the fridge. (JOANIE *groans at this. He turns a page)* Ah! And *this* one—TA-DA!—is "After." How it'll look after we've finished converting it into a nursery. *(Pause)* "Nursery." Yecch!

JOANIE: Let's just call it "the monster's lair."

BEN: So many bizarre new words to get used to! Like "prickly heat." Or "bonding"—they always talk about parent-child *bonding.* Sounds like you're caulking a bathtub.

JOANIE: Ben's a little tired of reading baby books.

BEN: And "quality time"—I *love* that one. That's time that, if it was being spent on you, you'd know you were getting screwed. *(He sets down the sketchbook)* And of course in the years ahead, we've got lots of *other* great expressions to look forward to. Like, "Hi, kids, I'm home!" Or who can forget *this* late-'50s classic: "Gee, kids, I don't know— *you'll have to ask your mother!*"

(JOANIE crosses to the pile of paints at right center to switch brushes)

JOANIE: *("Motherly")* "It's okay with me if it's okay with your dad."

BEN: "Your mom and I are going to take a little *nap* now—" *(He grabs her playfully, groping)*

JOANIE: Hey!

BEN: "—so pay no attention to those strange *sounds* you may hear."

JOANIE: Stop! You'll make me mess up! *(She goes back to the wall, trying to paint, but he's all over her)*

BEN: "That's just Daddy, strangling the cat."

JOANIE: Ben!

BEN: How 'bout it, Mom, wanna take a nap? Little *snooze,* maybe?

JOANIE: *(Trying to squirm away)* No, I don't!

BEN: *(To audience)* We're down to just one position now— but, fortunately, it's a *great* one.

(JOANIE *manages to break free of* BEN *and backs away, still holding her tray of paint*)

JOANIE: Ben! *Some* things can *stay* secret! *(He stalks her, occasionally reaching in for a grab. The game has taken on a bit of an uglier edge)*

BEN: C'mon, honey, fat girls are my favorite!

JOANIE: We have work to do! Stop it!

BEN: Screw the work! Father knows best! *(He jerks her tray and brush away, setting them down on the floor, then seizes her by the waist and kisses her. She shoves him away furiously)*

JOANIE: Father knows *least!* *(Pause)* Now c'mon, start painting!

BEN: Nag, nag, nag . . .

JOANIE: I mean it, Ben! I can't do this whole room by myself.

BEN: I'm helping! I'm helping . . . *(Long pause while they both try to regain composure. She picks up her tray and brush, goes back to painting the wall, right, around the window. He picks up his can of yellow paint, looks around restlessly)* I need a stick for this.

JOANIE: Stir it with a brush.

BEN: All the little hairs get clogged up. Down at the handle.

JOANIE: Well, stir it with just the tip, then.

BEN: No good. That won't reach the gunk on the bottom. Where's a stick? *(He roams about the room, searching)*

I need one of those massive tongue-depressor-type guys . . .

JOANIE: They're all in the other cans.

BEN: *(Pause)* I told you to pick up some more at the hardware.

JOANIE: No you didn't.

BEN: Yes I did, I distinctly asked you.

JOANIE: Well, then, I guess I forgot.

BEN: *(Irritated)* Great! Terrific! You forgot.

JOANIE: Ben, why make such a big deal?

BEN: I'm not making a big deal! I just think that if you're going to nag at a guy all his life about painting, then you might have the common courtesy to remember to get a couple of lousy sticks.

JOANIE: *(Growing angry herself)* Stir it with your hand, for all I care.

BEN: My hand? My *hand? (Pause)* Excuse me, wait a minute, but if we're going to *do* this, then let's do it right, okay? I mean, excuse me, but this was not my idea in the *first* place! It just so happens that *I* wanted a *circus* in here!

JOANIE: *(Mutters)* You *are* a circus.

BEN: What did you say?

JOANIE: *(Brightly)* Nothing!

BEN: No, wait a minute. Repeat what you just said.

JOANIE: Look in the kitchen, if it's so important to you. We may have some chopsticks.

BEN: *Chopsticks?*

JOANIE: Chopsticks! *(Screams)* CHOPSTICKS!

BEN: *(Pause; a bit awed)* Well, if we're going to stir the god-damned paint, then don't for Christ's sake tell me to stir it with just my *hand*, okay? *(She is silent)* I mean, I'm glad to help. But *Christ! (He exits through the swinging door, slapping it out of his way)*

JOANIE: Stir it with your *prick*, Ben. *(To audience)* Well, he fusses, he bothers, he gets underfoot, and he never *does* anything! You watch! By the time he finally gets that paint ready, he'll've thought up some *other* excuse. Anything to avoid seeing this room ever finished . . .

(She sets down her tray and brushes)

When is he going to stop *punishing* me for being pregnant? That's what I'd like to know. I mean, this didn't happen by spontaneous combustion!

(She crosses angrily to the ladder and yanks it up, swiveling it toward the up right corner, where she's been working. But the effort is too great, and abruptly she sags against the ladder with a little moan)

Ohh . . . Oh boy.

(She sits on a rung, puts her head down. Pause)

I'm sorry, I get so . . . dizzy sometimes . . .

(Another pause. She finally looks up. Quietly)

42

Let's *have* it, he said. So what if it's a surprise. We're as ready as we'll ever be—he *said* that. And now, because I was dumb enough to take him at his word, he'll never forgive me. *(Pause)* Ben is better at cleverness than at feelings. And I'm stronger than he is, I've always known that. *(She rises)* But even though I've been strong enough for both of us—when I had to be—I don't know if I can be strong enough for *three*. When the baby arrives, and I really need Ben to *be* there—what happens then? When I'm too tired or too depressed or just too damned pissed off to cope anymore, what's *he* going to do? Hide in the kitchen?

(BEN *opens the swinging door, sticks his head through*)

BEN: *(Angrily)* There's no chopsticks in here!

JOANIE: Did you look in all the drawers?

BEN: Which drawers?

JOANIE: By the fridge! Utensils.

BEN: Nobody can find a *thing* in here!

(He disappears again. JOANIE *crosses down center, looking anxiously at the audience)*

JOANIE: I'll tell you something, but you have to promise never to tell Ben. This weekend—at my parents'—I came within a hair of asking if I could move back in. But how do you say to your Mom and Dad, "I'm six months pregnant and I think maybe my marriage is ending . . . ?"

(From offstage, we hear a crash of pots and pans as BEN *begins ransacking the kitchen)*

I've asked myself a hundred times—what if I'm having this baby for all the wrong reasons? What if this is really just some ridiculous attempt to make Ben stop taking me for granted? Or what if I'm only going through with this because I can't keep a job? Or because it's trendy, or because my clock was ticking . . . I mean, *terrible* questions, and I've agonized over them for *weeks.*

(More crashes from the kitchen—drawers being yanked open and slammed shut. JOANIE *does her best to ignore this racket, but it drives her to greater urgency)*

Until this morning, coming back here on the Metroliner, when it suddenly occurred to me—somehow for the first time—that maybe . . . just maybe . . . I was having this kid because I actually *wanted* her. *(She smiles fiercely) I* wanted her—*me!* And if he won't—

*(*BEN *reenters, this time carrying an electric whisk, the cord trailing)*

BEN: *This* oughtta fix the sonofabitch . . . *(He crosses to the wall, right, kneels to plug the whisk into an electrical outlet)*

JOANIE: Ben—you can't—*(Laughs)*—you can't use that!

BEN: Why not?

JOANIE: Use a spatula, or a bread knife.

BEN: What the hell's wrong with this?

JOANIE: We're not making a meringue!

BEN: Why can't you let me do one thing my own way? Hmm? Why *is* that? I'm really interested to know.

JOANIE: Ben, I'm sorry—I don't mean to laugh, but the paint will get—

BEN: Is that so hard for you? Is that something that you find impossible to do?

JOANIE: The paint will get inside the works, and we'll never be able to clean it!

BEN: *(Rises, shouting)* So we'll throw it away and buy a new one! Big fucking deal! But don't keep telling me what to do!

JOANIE: *(Snaps) Give* me that! *(She grabs the whisk from his hands and stalks tensely into the kitchen. He follows her a few steps, as if to grab her arm, but then she's gone. He turns to the audience, livid)*

BEN: She's always right, and I'm always wrong! Okay? If you're keeping score, that's all you need to know.

(He paces angrily, kicking at the discarded stencils)

She's this sweet goddamn Earth Mother, so god-damned *put*-upon, and I'm just a spoiled immature selfish *prick* who only thinks about himself—okay? Knocks up his wife and then can't get behind the program—I mean, what the hell is *that?*

(Crossing downstage toward audience)

Except for one little thing—I'm the one who has to get *up* in the morning! Okay? I'm the one who goes off to work so we might have a little *money* around here, so we can pay for the fucking *kid's* twenty-two million dollars a *year* in college *tuition!*

(JOANIE reenters, carrying a spatula. She closes the door quietly and stands listening, shocked at his intensity. He hasn't yet seen her)

I'm the one who has to climb into that goddamn Sixth Avenue *meat* grinder every day, goddamn *trash*sports, knowing that if the goddamn ratings drop by half a point, it's my *ass!* Can you feature that? And *she's* the one—*(He turns, gesturing, and sees her)*

JOANIE: *(Pause; quietly)* Are we still talking about a paint stick?

(He takes a deep breath and plunges on, even louder)

BEN: —*She's* the one who sits around here doing her goddamned little drawings all day, goes off to do her volunteer work, has tea with the *girls,* for Christ's sake, and then says —*(He looks at his watch)*—"Oh, what the hell, I got some time to kill, I think I'll have a baby!" So you tell me—*(Then, to her) You* tell *me,* who's so fucking *selfish* around here?

JOANIE: Do you even know how pathetic that sounds?

BEN: I never wanted this kid! *Never!* And I don't want him now!

JOANIE: Liar! *(Throws the spatula)* LIAR!

BEN: Every fucking day you get bigger, and *we* get smaller! *Can't you understand?* I liked us the way we *were!*

JOANIE: Ben, you're trying to make me choose between you and the baby, and I can't *do* that anymore! You can't *ask* me to!

BEN: What the hell was I supposed to do? Knock you out and drag you to the abortion?

JOANIE: *(White, shaken)* You don't *say* that to me! You don't say to me something that can never be taken back!

BEN: *(Shouting)* A baby! A *baby* can never be taken back!

JOANIE: Get out of here. Just get out of this apartment . . .

BEN: No, hey, we've got some painting to do—remember?

(He crosses to the box of paints, down left. She follows, frightened)

JOANIE: I mean it, Ben! You're obviously hysterical, so just get out of my sight. I'll paint by myself.

(He rummages through the box, finding a can of black paint and a sponge brush. He pries the lid off the can with a screwdriver)

BEN: Oh no—no—we're having the baby together, let's paint the room together! Only, let's not do all these *birds* and rainbows and shit—all these cutesy little *butter-flies* . . .

JOANIE: What are you—Ben, no—stop it!

BEN: Let's paint some stuff our kid can really *learn* from, huh, Joan? What do you say? Let's surround this little fucker with the *real* facts of life!

(He starts for the wall, right. She tries to grab his arm, but he pulls away from her)

JOANIE: Ben, I'll scream! I swear to God—I'll wake the dead!

BEN: Oh, *I* know! *Here's* a good one!

JOANIE: Ben, *nooo* . . . !

(He hurries to the wall, dipping his brush, and paints a fat, ugly dollar sign over her butterfly)

BEN: You're never too young to learn *that* one . . .

(For a moment, JOANIE is almost too stunned to react. Then she begins to scream, again and again, pausing only to gasp for breath. He crosses to the far wall, left, shouting over her)

Or how about this? How about *this* for decoration?

(He paints the outline of a heart, then slashes a savage diagonal "break" across it)

A broken heart? Good to know? Or how about—oooh!—a big—fat—juicy—black—*mushroom cloud?!*

(Moving with frenzied jabs, he paints a huge mushroom cloud over JOANIE's rainbow. Then he hurls the brush against the floor furiously. He is gasping for breath. The anger drains out of him, as abruptly as it first came on, and he sags down to a sitting position on the floor. He looks numbly at the walls, the enormity of what he has done gradually settling over him. For a long moment, JOANIE is frozen, moaning softly. Then she crosses to gently touch the butterfly painting. She looks at the smear on her fingers, then in disbelief at BEN. Long pause)

BEN: *(Almost a whisper)* Mommy, Mommy . . . what is wrong with Daddy?

JOANIE: He's scared. *(Pause)* I'm scared too, baby.

(She moves to the ladder, pulling off and discarding her smock as she goes. She grabs her sweater from the ladder, then picks up her suitcase, down left. She pauses there, looking at him)

BEN: *(As she is moving)* Joanie, I'm sorry—I don't know why I did that. That was so stupid. We can fix it—we can paint it back. *(Growing more alarmed)* I'll make it just like it was, Joanie—I swear I will . . .

(She crosses past him, up to the french doors)

BEN: Joanie? We can fix it—?

JOANIE: Not this time, Ben.

(She exits through the french doors. After a moment we hear the front door opening and then closing)

BEN: *(Softly)* Joanie . . . ?

(BLACKOUT & CURTAIN)

END OF ACT ONE

ACT TWO

JOANIE: Men your age don't have heart attacks! (Anne Lange as Joanie and Mark Blum as Ben)

BEN: Lots of nice times, huh, Joanie? (Anne Lange as Joanie and Mark Blum as Ben)

CHARLOTTE: I'm afraid she might do something foolish. And tragic! (Jo Henderson as Charlotte and Thomas Toner as Gil)

JOANIE: Listen to me! We haven't got much time. (Anne Lange as Joanie and Mark Blum as Ben)

BEN: Look, maybe . . . maybe I'll just say goodbye to you. (Mark Blum as Ben)

The same room.

A Sunday afternoon in early spring.

The transformation from dining room to nursery is now complete. The walls have been painted over, a pale blue, or perhaps papered. No trace remains of Ben's vandalization, nor of the mural. There might be a framed child's poster or two. The window is cracked a few inches, but its protective gate is closed and padlocked. Lacy curtains have been added. The french doors have also been curtained, to allow more privacy. One of them is open partway as the act begins; we can catch a glimpse of the hallway bookcase.

There is a wicker bassinet on rollers, resting just now near the up right corner. Across from it, in the up left corner, is a large, sturdy crib with high sides. A small quilt is draped over the upstage railing of the crib. A large, colorful mobile is suspended from the ceiling over the crib. A chandelier may also have been added at center. We cannot see into the crib or the bassinet.

The room is densely furnished, in a sort of fussily delicate style. It's perfectly nice, and quite expensive-looking, but far from what we might consider Ben or Joanie's taste. Most of the furnishings are white. In the up right corner, just upstage of the bassinet, is a dresser. Its top has been covered with a plastic pad so that it can double as a changing surface. A wicker shelf unit hangs on the wall above the dresser, and its shelves—as well as the dresser drawers—are filled with disposable diapers, baby clothing, lotions, powders, tissues, cotton swabs, infant-care manuals, etc. A humidifier sits to one side of the dresser top, aimed toward the bassinet, and runs silently throughout the act. A plastic-lined wastebasket sits beside the dresser. Down right there is an upholstered chaise with throw pillows. Down left, a small table with a drawer or two. The cushioned rocking chair that would normally rest beside this table is instead, at the beginning of the act, pulled toward center. A pale oriental rug covers much of the floor.

Throughout the act, a party will be in progress offstage, centered in the living room. We'll hear snatches of voices, laughter, perhaps even music—amateurish exhibitions on a piano, for instance. These party noises are constant throughout, but generally rather muted; they grow louder whenever the french doors are opened, or the swinging door to the kitchen. (And, as in Act One, we are also aware of distant traffic noise whenever the window is open.) The attendance of a fairly large number of guests is indicated by the many overcoats piled onto the chaise, down right, as well as by the stack of wrapped gifts resting on top of, and even underneath, the small table down left. One gift, already partly unwrapped, sits on the rocking chair at center.

(Lights fade up slowly on JOANIE, *who stands staring fixedly into the crib. Low party noises in the background. She's in her stockinged feet, holding her shoes in one hand, and appears exhausted. Her elegant dress is disheveled, her hair tangled. A pause. Then abruptly she raises one of the shoes overhead and hurls it into the crib with a soft cry. The second shoe follows, with equal violence. She paces back and forth, upset, then goes to the rocking chair. She snatches up the gift box and sits. She rips out the tissue paper fiercely, throwing it on the floor, then takes out the gift. It is a pair of knitted baby booties [blue ones]. She stares at these for a few moments, then all at once bursts into tears. This lasts for only a few moments, after which she struggles to regain her composure. Another pause. Then* CHARLOTTE, *her mother, pokes her head through the open french door. She is a tense, sharp-eyed woman, fashionably dressed. She studies* JOANIE *suspiciously for a few moments, then enters, assuming a cheery*

manner. She carries a pair of overcoats and a small wrapped gift)

CHARLOTTE: Aunt Bonnie and Uncle Wallace have arrived! It's bound to be another spoon. *(She crosses to add this new gift to the stack on the small table, down left.* JOANIE *wipes her face furtively)* Why does everyone think they have to give *spoons?* We've got enough already to start a hootenanny band. *(Pause)* Have you got him to sleep yet?

JOANIE: See for yourself. (CHARLOTTE *hesitates a moment, trying to read this strange mood, then crosses over to the bassinet, looks down)*

CHARLOTTE: Oh, will you *look* at him! Precious little lamb . . . Look how he keeps smiling, even in his sleep . . .

(She crosses to the chaise, piling the new overcoats onto the rest)

Your father and I thought he was an angel in church this morning. A perfect little angel, right through the service!

(Ignoring her, JOANIE *crosses to the small table for another gift, then back to the rocker. She tears it open, joylessly discarding the wrapping.* CHARLOTTE *is rather annoyed by her inattention and messiness. She goes back to the bassinet)*

Dear—do you think it's wise to leave him in Gramma Spyvey's gown?

JOANIE: Why, what's the difference?

*(CHARLOTTE *reaches into the bassinet, lifting a corner of the baby's coverlet)*

CHARLOTTE: He's looking flushed. His poor little legs can't get any air.

JOANIE: He doesn't breathe through his legs.

CHARLOTTE: I know that, dear . . . All I'm suggesting is that Daniel might be more comfortable in one of his other outfits.

(JOANIE tosses aside the gift she's just opened, crosses to the table for another, then returns to her rocker)

JOANIE: He likes being swaddled. He finds it reassuring.

CHARLOTTE: What about that darling little terry thing I gave you? That might look nice . . . *(She pats JOANIE on the shoulder, then crosses to the table, opening a drawer)* Or his Ernie and Bert T-shirt, where did we put that—?

JOANIE: Mom, if you're worried he's gonna shit in your family heirloom, then why don't you just *say* so?

CHARLOTTE: *(Sharply)* There's no need to be coarse, Joanie. *(Pause)* Your great-grandmother's christening gown is China silk. It's very fragile. And yes, as a matter of fact, I would *not* appreciate his making a . . . mistake in it.

JOANIE: *(Loudly)* The word is "shit," Mom. Capital S-H-I-T. And it's not a mistake, he does it on purpose.

(Alarmed, CHARLOTTE goes to close the french doors. JOANIE launches into a sudden, savage outburst)

Why the hell does everything have to be a euphemism with you? Why can't you just once in your whole goddamn phony *life* call one thing by its real name?

(CHARLOTTE crosses stiffly to the table, makes some unnecessary adjustments to the pile of gifts)

Why? Why can't you do that? But no—people don't die, do they, Mom? No, they "pass on." And people don't go crazy, either! People don't go stark raving out of their fucking *gourds*—no, they go through a "phase." Isn't that what I heard you telling cousin Ruth? "Joanie's going through a little phase right now." A little *phase*, Mom? What the hell was—what was World War II—"a wee squabble"?

(CHARLOTTE *is startled and hurt by the intensity of this attack. For a moment she can think of nothing to say*)

CHARLOTTE: Well! I don't know what's gotten into *you* all of a sudden.

(JOANIE *laughs bitterly. She rises, crossing for another gift*)

JOANIE: Oh, let's think real hard, Mom. Let's put our heads together and think *real* hard, and see if maybe we can't come up with *some* reason why I might be just the *least* little bit bummed out today. (*She returns to the rocker, begins tearing into the gift*)

CHARLOTTE: (*Pause*) You didn't suppose—he'd actually have the gall to show up at the service? Surely not.

JOANIE: I don't know what I "supposed."

CHARLOTTE: Well, is that what you wanted?

JOANIE: (*Angrily*) I don't know!

CHARLOTTE: Ben is a very rude, very selfish young man. But even he has his limits, thank God. Your father would have had thrombosis.

JOANIE: It's Ben's baby too, Mom. (*She takes a silver rattle from the gift box, examines it, giving it a few bored shakes*)

CHARLOTTE: *(Fiercely) Was* his baby. *Could* have been his baby! . . . Any *earth*worm can be a father, Joanie. Any slug! But real parenting takes backbone, and Ben Marcus never had much. I'm sorry, but there it is.

(She snatches the rattle away from JOANIE, *then moves fretfully about, clearing up the discarded wrappings and throwing them into the wastebasket)*

I'm sure you must be upset. I'm sure you're tired. I'm tired too. But I don't think I've done anything to deserve being treated the way I have been these last few weeks. I'm only trying to help you, Joanie! I've given you an entire month of my time. I've decorated your nursery for you! I've arranged this wonderful party, just to try to take your mind off your troubles, and in return I get not one *iota* of thanks. Instead I get curses and nasty talk and sour looks. Well, I've had it! I've had it too! *(At the bassinet)* And I just hope you never get this same heartache from Daniel.

(Pause. Her housekeeping done, she turns briskly to JOANIE)

Now! Let's see if we can't keep ourselves looking smart, hmmm? Just for a *little* while longer. And fix your hair! Some of these people drove a long way to get here. Come on—up up up!

(She coaxes JOANIE *from her chair; then, once she's up, moves it back to her preferred location, down left near the small table)*

Thaaaat's good! Now. We'll pick something nice and fresh out of your closet, and then you'll feel *so* much better! What have you done with your shoes?

*(*JOANIE *is silent)*

Joanie . . . ? I asked you a question.

JOANIE: *(Hesitantly)* They're in the crib.

(CHARLOTTE *is startled. She crosses to the crib, looks in, then stares at* JOANIE)

CHARLOTTE: What on earth are they doing in there?

JOANIE: My feet hurt.

CHARLOTTE: But, sweetheart—why the *crib?*

JOANIE: *(Very quietly)* I don't know . . . (JOANIE *abruptly begins to sob. She crosses to the rocker, sits, burying her face in her hands.* CHARLOTTE *is further alarmed)*

CHARLOTTE: *(Pause)* Joanie . . . is there something you want to tell me?

(JOANIE *shakes her head)*

I mean about the baby. Anything at all?

(JOANIE *doesn't respond.* CHARLOTTE *moves closer)*

Look, I know you're feeling . . . well, a bit . . . blue. That's only natural. But after all, sweetheart, this was meant to be a celebration! So let's not let our friends see us —oh, you know—moping around with long faces. Or behaving . . . inappropriately. All right? Just because they've come here today under somewhat . . . unusual circumstances.

(JOANIE *can't help laughing at this. She looks up, wiping her eyes)*

JOANIE: The mother and father of the baby getting a divorce. Is that what you mean, Mom?

CHARLOTTE: *(Pause; gently)* "Unusual circumstances." *(Pause)* You will promise me you'll try, won't you, Joanie? You will at least—make an effort?

JOANIE: Oh, I'm liable to do *anything*, Mom. *(She rises)* Anything at all! I'm going through a "phase," remember?

(She surprises CHARLOTTE *with a quick, firm kiss on the cheek, then exits through the french doors, swaying a bit to the sound of the party music.* CHARLOTTE *hesitates for a moment, then goes fearfully to the crib. She takes another look down at* JOANIE's *shoes, reacting with a shudder. She backs away from the crib, uncertain what she should do next, then hurries out, following* JOANIE. *One of the french doors is left partly open.*

For several moments the room is empty. Then suddenly BEN's *head appears in the window. He is crouched on the fire escape, peering into the nursery. When he's certain the coast is clear, he tugs open the window. Then he reaches one arm in, below the gate bars, fumbling along the sill. The key to the gate's padlock hangs from a nail at one side of the sill. He locates this key, slips it off the nail, then unlocks the padlock. He removes this, setting it down on the fire escape, then swings open the gate. He climbs in through the window and stands beside it, catching his breath and listening warily.*

BEN *wears a suit and tie, and would look quite spiffy, had he not encountered a good deal of difficulty in scaling the fire escape. As it is, his hands, elbows, and shirt front are smudged with grime, his tie twisted askew, and his pants ripped over one knee. There's a cut on that knee and he walks with a bad limp. He wears a small nylon backpack over his suit jacket. He stands staring around the room, surprised— not altogether happily—by the extent of its transformation. He spots the crib, then slips his backpack off, dropping it on the chaise. He removes from it a couple of stuffed animal toys —a duck and a hand puppet. Glancing warily through the french doors, he crosses to the crib. He hesitates [a deep breath], then looks inside, expectantly displaying his gifts.*

His expression changes to a frown. Dropping the toys inside the crib, he takes out JOANIE's *shoes, turning them over in puzzlement. He glances around, and his eyes are caught by the bassinet. He crosses and looks inside it.*

His face lights up with wonder as he stares at his son. A long moment. He reaches to touch the baby, realizes he's still holding the shoes, and puts them into his coat pockets. Another nervous glance at the french doors. He decides to push the bassinet farther away from them, toward center, before spending time with the baby. But just as he does so, he hears someone approaching—and singing to himself—out in the hallway.

BEN *looks wildly about, uncertain where to hide, then races back to the window, snatching up his backpack as he goes. He climbs outside, pulling the gate shut behind him, and is just about to close the window when he freezes at the sight of* GIL, JOANIE's *father, entering through the french doors.*

GIL *is a heavyish man wearing a chef's apron over a gray suit. He faces the world with a sort of slightly bewildered geniality. Just now he is crooning ["Danny Boy"] and carrying a tray on which sit three empty champagne bottles and some wadded cocktail napkins. He concentrates so hard on the balance of this tray that he doesn't see* BEN, *who is clearly outlined in the window. As* GIL *crosses the room, he pauses to peek fondly into the bassinet, which now rests at center)*

GIL: *(Sings)* "It's I'll be therrre, in sunshine and in sha-aa-dow . . . Oh, Danny Boy—oh, Danny Boy—I love you soooo . . ." *(He blows a kiss, then exits into the kitchen, still humming happily and concentrating on his tray's balance)*

(BEN *shuts the window and drops down out of sight on the fire escape in the next instant, just as* CHARLOTTE *reappears at the french doors, carrying two more overcoats and another gift—evidently, from its size, yet another spoon. She is just in time to see* GIL *disappearing through the swinging door, before she herself must turn back, speaking to someone in the hallway)*

CHARLOTTE: —No, no, dear—we don't want a lot of strange bacteria coming into the nursery. *(Pause)* Well, I didn't mean it *per*sonally, Midge. We'll bring him back out in just a few minutes, alright? *(She smiles charmingly to disengage herself, then shuts the doors and rushes over to the swinging door, pushing it slightly open. An urgent whisper)* Gil! Come *here!* Gil!

GIL: *(Off)* Those cheese puffs come out of the oven in five minutes, Clara. Make sure you keep them—

CHARLOTTE: *(Slaps door impatiently)* Gilbert!

(GIL *reenters, now carrying a plate of assorted canapés)*

GIL: What! What is it?

(CHARLOTTE *pulls* GIL *by the arm away from the kitchen door, then motions dramatically)*

CHARLOTTE: Look in the crib! *(He crosses, puzzled, does so. She goes to the chaise with her coats)* You see them?

GIL: Mmm-hmm.

CHARLOTTE: Joanie put them there. She *admits* it!

GIL: *(Mildly)* I expect he wanted something to play with. *(He samples one of his canapés)*

62

CHARLOTTE: *(Surprised)* To *play* with? I'd hardly call those suitable toys.

GIL: You think they're too big for him?

CHARLOTTE: *(Severely)* This is no time for your jokes!

(He shrugs, picks out another canapé and eats it. She lays out her overcoats on the pile, smoothing them down irritably)

God *knows* what sort of germs those things've got on them. Germs and dog mess. And pointy edges!

GIL: Dog mess? *(Mystified, he looks back in the crib)*

(CHARLOTTE crosses to the bassinet, still holding the gift)

CHARLOTTE: Poor little angel. Woojy woojy . . . She's been acting very peculiar, Gil. Very peculiar indeed. I don't like it.

GIL: *(Eating another canapé)* What do you mean, "peculiar?"

CHARLOTTE: Will you stop eating? This is serious! *(She snatches the plate from him)*

GIL: Sorry.

(She crosses to the small table to put down the gift, then up to the dresser to put down the canapé plate)

CHARLOTTE: Sudden tears. Violent temper tantrums! Forgetfulness. Imaginary noises! She handled him in church this morning like he was some kind of bean bag. And now those—those *things* in his crib! I'm telling you, Gil—you look into that girl's eyes and there's no joy there, no sparkle. You haven't *been* here, you don't know what it's *like*.

(Crossing back to bassinet) And what happens tomorrow, after I'm gone? She'll be all alone here with this baby, and I'm just afraid she might . . . . *(Stops herself)*

GIL: Might what?

CHARLOTTE: *(Taking his arm)* Alright, I'll say it! I'm afraid she might do something foolish. And tragic! Not on *purpose*, Gil, I'm not suggesting that! But accidentally—when she's not herself.

GIL: Aren't you getting a bit carried away? *(He pats her reassuringly, then crosses to the dresser to retrieve his canapés)*

CHARLOTTE: These things *happen!* It's no use pretending they're only in the newspapers! That girl over in Glenloch left hers in the washing machine, and they didn't find the poor little thing till after the spin cycle.

GIL: *(Exasperated)* But it's only a couple of stuffed animals!

CHARLOTTE: Stuffed . . . what are you *talking* about? *(She crosses, reaching into the crib, then freezes. Confused, she comes out with one of BEN's toys)* She must've snuck back in here somehow and exchanged them! But—how could she . . . *(Pause)* Oh, Gil. I'm scared. *(She drops the toy back into the crib with a shudder)* What's happening to our little girl?

GIL: Charlotte—would you like to lie down for a bit? Here— let me clear away some of these coats . . .

CHARLOTTE: Her shoes were *in* there, not five minutes ago! I *saw* them.

GIL: Her *shoes?*

64

CHARLOTTE: Both of them!

GIL: *(Very puzzled)* What would her *shoes* be doing in Danny's crib?

CHARLOTTE: She put them there, silly. I just *told* you!

GIL: *(Slight pause)* Why would she do a thing like that?

CHARLOTTE: I don't *know* why! That's what we're trying to establish! Honestly, talking to you sometimes is like—wading through oatmeal!

GIL: Well, did she say anything? What did she say?

CHARLOTTE: *(Reluctantly)* She seemed hurt because . . . Ben didn't come this morning.

GIL: *(An angry roar)* Ben! If it wasn't for *that* sorry bastard, she wouldn't be alone in this mess in the first place!

CHARLOTTE: Keep your voice down!

GIL: *Ben . . . !*

(She crosses anxiously to the french doors, peeks out through the curtain. He sits on the end of the chaise, disgruntled, and eats another canapé)

CHARLOTTE: It's not enough that she married the wrong man, and then kept us waiting for eight years. *(Motioning to the bassinet)* It's not enough that she's practically a . . . an unwed mother! Now she's got to put us through this, too!

GIL: Aw now damn it, Charlotte, is that fair? *(Slight pause)* Look . . . she hasn't gotten four hours of uninterrupted sleep in the last month. Maybe she's just tired. You know—absentminded. Couldn't it just be that?

CHARLOTTE: Gil, she is severely depressed! Those shoes were meant as a *message*, can't you see that? "Somebody stop me, before it's too late!" *(Pause)* Talk to her, Gil! Draw her out. You know she'll never say anything important to me.

GIL: *(Sighs)* Where is she, the bedroom?

(CHARLOTTE shakes her head; she doesn't know)

Okay . . . okay, look—you try to keep the rest of them occupied. Just act normally. And *don't panic! (He hands her his plate)* Here—give them these. *(He exits through the french doors, taking off his apron as he goes. She goes to the bassinet, rolls it gently back up right, near the humidifier)*

CHARLOTTE: Don't you worry, sweetheart. Poor little peanut . . . Nana's still here. You're safe with Nana . . . *(She smiles to the baby, then turns to go back to the living room with the plate. Glancing at it, she is exasperated to see that GIL has left only two or three canapés uneaten. She crosses fretfully to the swinging door and exits)*

(After a few beats, BEN looks in again from the fire escape. He stands, pulls up the window, and pushes the gate wide open. Then he climbs back into the room, looking around cautiously. After another lingering, admiring glance into the bassinet, he limps up to the french doors. He listens, hears no one coming, and ventures a peek through them. After this he crosses to the swinging door, listens at it for a moment, then opens it just a crack to look inside. Mistake! He instantly lets the door close, then flattens himself against the wall beside it. The door opens again, and CHARLOTTE pokes her head out, puzzled. Did she see something just now? She can't be sure, and BEN is hidden from her by the angle of the door.)

Her attention is caught by the open window. She comes all the way into the room, carrying the refilled canapé plate)

CHARLOTTE: *(Softly)* Joanie . . . ?

(BEN, *eyes wide in alarm, is now fully revealed behind her, but her gaze is fixed on the window. She crosses to it slowly, with mounting concern. Along the way she pauses to look into the bassinet, reassuring herself that the baby is safe. She sets her plate down on the dresser. At the window, she touches the gate, swinging it softly on its hinges. Then she looks outside. Finally she leans all the way out to look down through the fire escape.*

With CHARLOTTE's *whole upper body hidden from sight,* BEN *tiptoes toward the french doors, attempting to escape, but then sees someone approaching in the hall and has to hurry back to the swinging door. He has just grabbed this open [the door has both a push plate and a small pull knob, which* BEN *now holds], masking himself behind it, when* JOANIE *appears at the french doors.*

JOANIE *is wearing a new dress and has also made an effort to repair her makeup and hair. She's still in her stockinged feet. She is far more cheerful now, in fact almost unnaturally exhilarated)*

JOANIE: Mom?

(CHARLOTTE *gives a little shriek, spins around, out of the window, to face her. She is holding the padlock in one hand, the key still inside it. She hides this behind her back)*

Is something wrong?

CHARLOTTE: Wrong? Ah . . . no!

JOANIE: Reverend Weeboldt just spilled clam dip all over his lap! I hope we have some seltzer left . . .

(She exits through the open kitchen doorway, still talking, as BEN *strains back against the wall.* CHARLOTTE *stares at the padlock, puzzled and frightened, and then back at the open window. From offstage)*

You know you were right? I feel so much better, just from changing clothes! I splashed a little water on my face . . . thanks, Clara . . . ran a comb through my hair . . . and all of a sudden . . .

(She reenters, carrying a seltzer bottle and a sponge, strikes a pose)

I'm a new woman! *(Slight pause)* God, it's weird how fast your moods can change sometimes, you know? *(Shrugs happily)* Just postpartum, I guess!

(She starts toward the living room, stops herself abruptly)

Why'd you open the window?

CHARLOTTE: *I* opened the window?

JOANIE: Mom, who else? (JOANIE *sets down the seltzer and sponge on the dresser, then takes a comforter from the top drawer. She rolls the bassinet toward center, farther from the window, then tucks the comforter over the baby)*

CHARLOTTE: Ummm . . . yes! I opened the window because . . . I thought the baby was too hot. Yes! Too hot in Gramma Spyvey's gown.

JOANIE: Well, you better close it. It's freezing out. *(She picks up her sponge and seltzer again)*

CHARLOTTE: Close it! Right!

JOANIE: There's a terrible draft through here. *(She goes to the kitchen door and gives it a casual tug, then crosses to bend over the crib, looking for her shoes.* CHARLOTTE, *moaning softly to herself, turns to shut the window, then the gate. She slips the padlock back in place, trying to conceal this move from* JOANIE, *but fumbling in her nervousness)*

(The kitchen door swings briskly closed, revealing BEN—*but for a split second both women are still focused elsewhere. He has a moment of utter panic before the door's rebound swing carries its pull knob magically back into his hand, and he's once again concealed.*

JOANIE, *puzzled, straightens up from the crib holding one of* BEN's *stuffed animals—the puppet)*

JOANIE: Hey, what's this?

CHARLOTTE: *(Turns)* That? Why . . . that's a *toy*, dear.

(Shifting her sponge and seltzer under one arm, JOANIE *slips the puppet on her hand)*

JOANIE: I never saw this one before . . . What've you done with my shoes?

*(*CHARLOTTE *tries to laugh, though it comes out as more of a groan.* JOANIE *crosses to her)*

Mom, are you sure you're okay? *(Slyly, making the puppet "talk")* "We could get you a Miltown!"

CHARLOTTE: No, no! I'm fine! *(She smiles, much too heartily, then turns back to the window to snap the padlock shut. She pockets the key)* See? Fine! Right as rain!

JOANIE: There's a whole pile of junk in the medicine cabinet I'm not supposed to take while I'm nursing. Let me see what I can find. (JOANIE *exits through the french doors, tossing the puppet back into the crib as she goes.* CHARLOTTE *crosses to the bassinet, looks at the baby. All at once a new and ghastly danger occurs to her*)

CHARLOTTE: Medicine cabinet! *(She rushes out after* JOANIE, *leaving the french doors ajar)*

(A beat of silence, and then BEN *cautiously closes the kitchen door. He tiptoes to the french doors, peeks out through them, then closes them quietly. He unslings his backpack as he crosses to the dresser. He sets down the pack and opens it. With quick, nervous movements he removes a bottle of wine [kosher, with a screw top], a silver kiddush cup, a book, and a yarmulka. He puts the yarmulka on his head, securing it with a bobby pin, then puts the book under his arm and unscrews the wine bottle. He starts toward the bassinet, pouring the wine into the cup. He screws the top back on the bottle, sets it on the floor, then, holding the wine cup under his chin, uses both hands to flip through the book till he's found his place. Taking the cup in hand, he stands looking nervously down at the baby for a few moments. Then he begins reading aloud, quickly but quietly, sometimes stumbling a bit over pronunciations)*

BEN: *(Reads)* "*Baruch ata Adonai Elohainu melech ha'olam asher kidshanu b'mitz-votav v'tzivanu . . . v'tzivanu . . . l'hakniso bivrito . . . shel Avraham avinu.* (Raise glass over baby)." *(He does as instructed)* "*K'shem sheh'nichnas labrit, ken . . .* something *l'Torah . . . u'le'chupah* something something . . ." *(He drinks from the glass, then raises it over the baby again)* "*Kayaim es hayeled . . . hazeh ben'Yisrael . . . Dahnyiel ben Binyamin . . .*" *(Pause)* "Let his—let his name be called in Israel, 'Daniel' . . . the son of Benjamin." *(Pause. He drinks again, then smiles down at the baby, deeply moved. He sets the prayer book down inside the bassinet, then dips a finger into the wine. He reaches to touch it to the baby's lips) Mazel tov, kiddo . . .*

(Abruptly the baby makes a loud shriek, which turns immediately into crying. BEN *jumps)* Sshhh! *Sssshhhh . . . !*

(He dips his fingers again, flicks more wine toward the baby. No good. Setting the glass down on the floor, he makes funny faces, bobbing up and down. No good. He hurries to the crib, pulls out his toy duck, makes it dance for the baby while he supplies quacking noises. But despite BEN's *desperate efforts, the baby only wails louder and louder.* BEN *throws the duck back into the crib, looks around in a panic. He grabs up the book and bottle, then races to the dresser for his backpack. These in hand, he rushes to the window, tugging at the gate. To his horror, he realizes the gate is locked and the key missing. He lunges for the padlock, rattling it futilely. The baby continues to screech. He hurries back to the dresser, opens one of the lower drawers, and shoves in his backpack, bottle, and book. He turns, sees the cup of wine still sitting on the floor, picks this up and drains it as he moves toward the chaise. Excited voices can be heard approaching in the hall)*

JOANIE: *(Off)* That's alright, Mom—I can figure this one out—

CHARLOTTE: *(Off)* No, no, dear, let me do it—

JOANIE: *(Off)* This is a strange cry—I don't understand it—

CHARLOTTE: *(Off)* Oh, I'm sure he just wants some company—

*(*BEN *flips the empty cup under the chaise, then his eyes dart around the room frantically. He takes a running start, then vaults into the empty crib, disappearing from our view. He*

reaches up for the quilt, draped over the railing, and yanks this down over himself in the same instant that JOANIE *enters through the french doors. As she hurries to the bassinet, she is followed closely by an anxious* CHARLOTTE. GIL *trails the two women, a helpless observer. The women talk rapidly, overlapping each other)*

JOANIE: No, no, something must have startled him—

CHARLOTTE: *(To the baby)* You're just lonesome in here, aren't you, sweetheart?

(JOANIE pulls the comforter off the baby, but before she can pick him up, CHARLOTTE has pushed her out of the way)

JOANIE: Mom, if you make a big fuss over him, you're just—

CHARLOTTE: He wants to go *right* out to the living room—

JOANIE: —you're just going to make it worse!

CHARLOTTE: —and meet all his nice new friends! Don't you, Danny!

JOANIE: *(Trying to get at the baby)* Mom, what are you *doing?*

CHARLOTTE: *(Blocking her)* I'm *taking* him to the *living* room! His nap is *over!*

(A sort of elaborate waltz develops, with CHARLOTTE trying to spin the bassinet away from JOANIE, and JOANIE pursuing it. The baby, now being rolled in circles, keeps squalling)

JOANIE: Give me a chance to see what's *wrong* with him first!

CHARLOTTE: Aunt Bonnie hasn't *seen* him yet!

JOANIE: She doesn't want to *see* him with his *face* all smunched up!

CHARLOTTE: She *loves* a smunched-up face! Now, *stop this!*

JOANIE: Mom, if you'll just leave me *alone* with him, I know how to make him *quiet!*

(CHARLOTTE *comes to a halt, facing* JOANIE, *with the bassinet at her back*)

CHARLOTTE: That's what I'm *afraid* of! *(To* GIL, *a loud whisper) Talk to her!*

(She wheels the bassinet out through the french doors and down the hall. JOANIE *follows her to the doorway in amazement, then stares back at her embarrassed father. From offstage, we hear the collective "AHHHHHH!" of the party guests seeing the baby. This is followed by a scattering of applause. The crying has faded away.* JOANIE *shuts the french doors. A slight pause)*

JOANIE: Dad . . . have you noticed that Mom is a little weird lately?

GIL: *(Chuckles uncomfortably)* Well, I— I think maybe we're all just a little bit weird lately—don't you?

*(JOANIE *crosses away from the doors, folding the baby's comforter)*

JOANIE: She came into the bathroom just now, pushed me out of her way, and started stuffing all the medicines into a pillowcase! When I asked her what she was doing, she said "You can't be too careful."

GIL: Well, she probably thought—one of the guests might get into them and leave something, uh, lying around . . . that

73

the baby might find and . . . eat. *(Pause)* Something like that.

JOANIE: Dad, the baby's a month old! He doesn't go foraging in the bathroom. She's totally nuts! *(She crosses to the dresser, puts the comforter away in the top drawer)*

GIL: *(Lamely)* That's how your mother shows her love for you.

JOANIE: How? By freaking out?

GIL: Maybe so, yes! Did you think there was some ideal way? *(Pause. He goes to her)* Don't be so tough on her. She's never been a grandmother before. She's got a lot to learn yet. You know what I'm saying?

JOANIE: *(Pause)* You're saying that I do too.

GIL: Joanie . . . sit down for a second.

(She crosses reluctantly to the chaise, sits on the end, among the coats. He sees the canapé plate on the dresser, where CHARLOTTE *left it, and goes to get it)*

GIL: Sandwich?

JOANIE: No, thanks.

GIL: C'mon, try the egg salad. I put a little curry in it. *(She takes one of the finger sandwiches, bites into it without much interest. He takes one for himself and eats it, standing awkwardly beside her)* You know, hon—Mom is kinda hurt you're making her move out tomorrow. She's only been here a month.

JOANIE: I'm sorry, Daddy. It's just impossible.

GIL: Well, if you won't give your Mom another try—

JOANIE: No! She's driving me—

GIL: —and I'm not suggesting that again!—then I wish you'd at least consider taking in a roommate.

JOANIE: Did you ever try to get somebody to room with a newborn? *(He is silent)* And besides—we've already been over this a hundred times. What're you really trying to say?

GIL: *(Sighs)* Okay. *(He looks around, sees the rocking chair, over by the small table. He crosses for it, bringing it back near* JOANIE*)* There *is* something that's been bothering me. I don't mean just today . . . *(He sits, holding the canapé plate on his lap. Brief pause)* Joanie . . . Joanie, when you were born, I was just out of the service . . . Your mom and I were still up in Ithaca, wondering what the hell we were ever gonna *do* with our lives. We were just a couple of dumb kids, really. Get married, have a baby right away, worry about it later . . . That's just how it was then. We bought your old crib there—*(He looks at it, smiles)*—I remember it cost $19.95 and we had to split the payments . . . But Joanie, the day you came home from the hospital—that had to be the proudest—and the happiest day of my whole life. I looked at you in that crib and thought, "Oh Jesus, she's so tiny, and we have so far to go together . . ." And I thought my heart would burst—would literally *burst* —from the joy I felt. *(Pause)* Still feel. *(Pause)* And Joanie, the thing of it is—the thing of it is that in all this time since Danny was born—I don't think I've even once heard you say you were happy to have him. That's all, just—happy. *(Pause)* And that to me is one hell of a thing.

JOANIE: *(Pause)* You too, huh?

GIL: Me too what?

JOANIE: Everybody here today seems obsessed with my happiness. It's like they're all pointing some kind of smile-ometer at me, and if the little needle doesn't stay over against the red mark, then I'm a lousy mother. *(Pause)* The baby ended my marriage, Dad! How happy should I be?

GIL: *(Gently)* I'm sure he didn't do it on purpose, Joanie.

JOANIE: *(Pause)* You're right. That's not fair. I was the one with all the expectations, not him . . . *(Pause)* Oh, Dad, Danny was going to be this great creative project for me—better than any painting I could ever do. He was going to make up for so many things in my life that I've screwed up . . . chickened out of . . . walked away from. But most of all, he was going to bring some new kind of magic to me and Ben. I wasn't quite clear on the details, but I just—I just knew he would *do* that . . . *(Fighting tears)* I've lost him, Daddy. I've really lost him . . .

GIL: Joanie—

JOANIE: He doesn't love me anymore! Don't you see? If he did he would've come today. He would've come in spite of everything . . . !

(BEN *peeks up cautiously over the edge of the crib.* GIL's *back is to him, and* JOANIE's *view of him is partially blocked by* GIL. BEN *watches her closely)*

But I was too proud to give him another chance, and now he's . . . he's really . . . Oh, Daddy . . . *(She sobs)*

GIL: Sweetheart, don't cry . . . Your Mom and I love you so much, Joanie . . . *(He tries to comfort her. She is embarrassed to have broken down in front of him)*

JOANIE: I know you do . . . And I'll make it somehow. *(She gets up, wiping her face, and crosses to look at the pile of gifts on the small table.* BEN *ducks down out of sight)* I may get a little depressed sometimes, but at least I still have Danny . . .

GIL: *(Hesitates)* Your mother says you . . . threw your shoes into his crib.

JOANIE: *(Surprised)* Is that what all this is about—my *shoes?*

GIL: Pointy edges, she said. Dog mess! You're still not wearing them.

JOANIE: *(Laughs with relief)* Dad, that was—that was nothing! I can't believe you guys have built that up into some whole big—look, the *baby* was in the *bassinet* . . . ! *(She moves upstage toward the dresser, indicating the normal position of the bassinet)* My *feet* were killing me, so I took my shoes off and threw them away! Big deal! *(She crosses to the crib, demonstrating)* I knew all *along* he wasn't—*(She turns, looking down, and freezes, seeing* BEN*)*—in the crib.

*(*BEN*'s hand appears, holding up her shoes, trying to be helpful. Numbly she accepts them.* GIL, *seated in the rocker and facing downstage, doesn't see this. He is preoccupied with selecting one of the canapés from his plate)*

GIL: Well, you've got to admit, hon, it's still a kinda peculiar thing to do. And then, later on, when your mother wanted to show them to me, they were gone. Vanished, into thin air!

*(*BEN*'s hands reach up again, snatching back the shoes.* JOANIE *spins around, still rigid with shock, and blocks as much of the crib as she can with her body.* GIL *eats the canapé calmly)*

Your mother was plenty upset, I can tell you. And then there was some kind of strange business with the window

—I didn't quite catch what the hell *that* was all about—*(He rises, curious to examine the window)*

JOANIE: Dad—I wonder if I might be alone now for a while.

GIL: *(Surprised)* What?

JOANIE: *(Harshly)* Please go away. Right now.

GIL: Joanie . . . what is it? *(He starts toward her, still holding the plate)* You look like you've just seen a—

JOANIE: No! Stay away!

(She springs for the rocking chair, snatching it up and using it to ward him off)

Don't come near me! *(He freezes)* I don't *mean* don't come near *me*. I mean you *could* come near *me* and that would be okay. I just mean don't come near . . . anything *else*.

(He stares at her, aghast. She looks down at the chair in her hands, takes a stab at nonchalant laughter)

This must look—you must think—Daddy, I'm *not crazy!* Ha ha ha! No!

(She crosses down left with the rocker, replaces it by the small table)

I just need some time alone in here to—to—

(She looks around desperately)

Sort these *coats* out! I mean, just look at them!

(She crosses to the chaise, half tugging him along, away from the crib)

These coats are a *mess!* How's anybody supposed to find their coat at the bottom of a pile like this?

GIL: Ah! *(Pause)* I better get your mother . . . *(He starts toward the kitchen, but she hurries after him, alarmed)*

JOANIE: *No! (She grabs his arm, spinning him around. He barely avoids spilling his plate. He stares at her wildly)*

GIL: Sweetheart—what—what—why—

JOANIE: Oh, just GET OUT! *(Shouts)* GET OUT! *GET OUT! (She hustles him all the way up to the french doors, ignoring his protests, then gives him a firm shove down the hall, toward the living room)* And tell *Mom* to stay away from me too! *(She stands in the doorway for a moment, making sure that GIL won't return. Then she quickly shuts the doors and sags against them, trying to collect herself. A pause)*

BEN: *(Still hidden)* Smoothly done.

(She rushes to the crib, slapping the side of it angrily)

JOANIE: You *bastard!*

(BEN sits up, looks at her indignantly)

BEN: Hey!

(As he stands, she grabs the railing of the crib and hauls on it with all her weight, trying to tip it over. It rocks but doesn't fall. They speak in harsh whispers)

JOANIE: You lousy—god-damned—

BEN: Joanie—stop it!

79

(She circles the crib, slapping at him. He fends off her blows with his hands)

JOANIE: —miserable—sneaking—

BEN: Ow! Stop hitting me!

(She flings a leg over the railing, climbs in with him. They square off like two boxers in an impossibly small ring)

JOANIE: —sonofabitch *bastard!* I *hate* you!

BEN: Fine! Terrific! Now will you please just—

JOANIE: Get out of this crib.

(Like a small child who won't be budged, he sits down, stubbornly grasping the railings)

BEN: No!

JOANIE: Get out of this *crib!*

BEN: Not till you calm down!

(She grabs his leg, trying to pull him free of the railing)

JOANIE: For once in your life, God damn it—

BEN: Joanie, if you'll just let me—

JOANIE: —stand up and take it like a *man!*

(She grabs up one of her shoes from the bottom of the crib and uses it to smack at his hands. She misses the first one, but connects solidly with the second [upstage] hand)

BEN: *(On her action)* Joanie, if you'll just let—hey!—if you'll please just let me explOWWWWWW . . . !

(He shrieks, holding his hurt hand, and slides down out of sight in the crib. Suddenly a bit anxious, she pauses in her attack)

JOANIE: Ben . . . ? Did that hurt you?

BEN: *(Gallantly)* No . . . I'm okay . . .

JOANIE: Well, how about . . . *this? (She throws away the shoe—into the corner, upstage of the crib—and swings a roundhouse punch down toward his head. We can't see the contact, but we hear it. He groans, and one of his legs flies upright in pain, the foot landing and hooking on the crib rail. She grabs her own fist, rocking with pain)* OWWWWW! *(Pause. Realizing his silence, she looks down at him)* Ben? *(Pause. Now genuinely worried)* Ben . . . ? *(She reaches into the crib, tries to slap him back to alertness. No luck)* Oh no. Oh *damn* it . . . ! *(She looks around the room, wondering what to try next. Finally she climbs out of the crib and rushes into the kitchen. She is gone for several seconds, leaving us with the incongruous image of* BEN's *shoe propped on the railing)*

(At last she returns, carrying a glass pitcher half filled with water. She goes to the crib, hesitates, then throws the water on BEN. *She leans in, checking the results. Evidently unsatisfied, she turns as if to go back to the kitchen for more water. But just as she reaches the swinging door,* CHARLOTTE *and* GIL *enter through it, forcing her backward.* JOANIE *is startled, still a bit breathless. She retreats toward the chaise, while they pause downstage of the crib, reluctant to get too close to her. Their attention is so fixed on her that they don't see* BEN's *foot. She hasn't noticed it either)*

JOANIE: Mom! Dad! There you are! I—finished with the coats . . . *(They glance past her to the coats, which are heaped as messily as ever)* And I was just about to, ah—water the plants! *(Slight pause)* You know, my *house*work has gone straight to hell since the baby was born. Have you noticed that? I know I shouldn't worry about it, I mean, it's not really important, but, welllll, you know me, Miss Spic-'n'-Span! Miss Neat-'n'-Tidy! Can't have our guests looking at a sloppy apartment, can we? A sloppy apartment means a sloppy mother!

CHARLOTTE: *(Pause)* What plants?

JOANIE: Well, there you are! That's just it! They all *died* because I never watered them! Did I say "plants?" No, no, what I *meant* was, water the guests. Offer the guests some water! That's what I meant.

GIL: *(Pause)* What water?

(CHARLOTTE crosses to her with elaborate caution and gently takes away the pitcher)

CHARLOTTE: Joanie . . . don't be alarmed. Your father and I understand what you're going through.

(JOANIE sits weakly on the chaise)

JOANIE: Oh, if only you did . . .

CHARLOTTE: *(Stroking her hair)* We want you to lie down in your bedroom—just for a little while—maybe turn the lights off—and just stay nice and cozy and calm . . .

(GIL crosses to CHARLOTTE's side. His move leaves BEN's foot completely exposed, and JOANIE sees it)

GIL: Just until Dr. Latimer gets here.

(CHARLOTTE glares at him, and he realizes his error. JOANIE rises hastily, gets between her parents and the crib, then backs up against its side)

JOANIE: Mom—Dad—look—I know what you're thinking. And you're only trying to help. *(Suddenly shrieks)* AGGGGHHHH! *(She points over their shoulders, as if she's seen something frightening in the window. They turn, startled, and while they're looking away, she shoves* BEN*'s foot off the railing, then leans against it, striking a casual pose. They turn back, stare at her)* But there's nothing wrong with me.

GIL: *(Looks at* CHARLOTTE, *appalled)* Of course not. What a thought!

JOANIE: I'm not crazy!

CHARLOTTE: No one said you were, sweetheart.

JOANIE: Then, why are you soothing me?

GIL: *(Soothingly)* Nobody is soothing you . . . !

JOANIE: There—you did it again!

CHARLOTTE: *(Slaps his arm)* Quit soothing her, Gilbert! *(Pause)* Do as we say, Joan. You may be a mother now, but you're still our little girl, too, and we expect to be obeyed. *(Pause)* Your father is prepared to use physical restraint. (GIL *looks at* CHARLOTTE, *alarmed; he's prepared to use no such thing.* JOANIE *realizes, though, that further resistance is futile. She takes a deep breath, offers a silent prayer that* BEN *won't be found, then exits through the french doors without looking back.* GIL *follows her to the doorway, watches her go down the hall)* She's getting worse!

GIL: *Think* of something!

CHARLOTTE: I'm *trying!* Can't you see I'm trying? Oh, if only we didn't have all these *people* here! *(She starts to the kitchen to get rid of the pitcher)* I can't believe I agreed to this party.

GIL: Agreed to it? It was your idea!

CHARLOTTE: *(Stops) Mine?!*

GIL: *(Goes to her)* You wanted to show everybody we weren't ashamed of the divorce, remember? You wanted to prove we had nothing to hide! *(His voice rising)* You think Joanie wanted this god-damned charade? You think *I* did?

CHARLOTTE: Then, you should have talked me out of it! *(She thrusts the pitcher into his arms, then stalks out through the french doors)*

GIL: *(Mutters)* Oh, *that'll* be the day . . . *(He exits into the kitchen)*

(The stage is deserted and silent for a long beat, then we hear a protracted groan from within the crib. BEN's hand appears on the railing, and after a moment he hauls himself upright. His head and shoulders are soaked. He peers nervously around the room, then climbs unsteadily from the crib. His legs have gone rubbery and he's more than a bit dazed. He reaches to feel his aching head, and his hand comes away holding the yarmulka. He looks at this ruefully for a moment, then lurches over to the chest of drawers. He drops the yarmulka into a drawer, takes out his wine bottle, twists off the cap, and drinks deeply. He winces at the sweetness, choking a little bit, then recaps the bottle and drops it back in the drawer.

His eye is caught by the window. He limps over to it and examines the lock, giving it a yank or two. He is still puzzled as to where the key could be. He looks around, then drops down to all fours, searching the floor.

84

After a few moments of this, JOANIE *enters through the french doors, sneaking quickly but very quietly. She slips up behind him)*

JOANIE: *(Whispers)* Ben!

BEN: NnnGAAAAAAAAHH . . . ! *(He pops to his knees in fright, but she moves quickly to clap her hands over his mouth, kneeling behind him)*

JOANIE: Listen to me! We haven't got much time. They think I'm in bed . . . *(He makes muffled sounds)* I'm going to take my hands away, but don't make any loud noises, okay? *(Pause) Okay? (He nods. She cautiously uncovers his mouth)*

BEN: Don't hit me again!

JOANIE: Oh, Ben—I thought I killed you! *(She startles him with an impulsive hug, then runs her hands anxiously over his head and shoulders)* Are you sure you're okay? Nothing is broken . . . ?

BEN: Joanie, we're alone! I can't believe it! I can't believe I'm actually touching you again . . .

JOANIE: *(Pulling away, rising)* What are you *doing* here?

BEN: You invited me!

JOANIE: To the *church,* Ben! I invited you to the *church!*

BEN: Yeah, well . . . I didn't really want to see your folks. *(He crosses to shut the french doors)* And I had a pretty good idea they didn't want to see me, either. *(Making "headlines" with his hands)* "Kooky Kike Crashes Christening!" "Episcopalians Pee in Plaid Pants!"

JOANIE: Oh, that's just great. That's real cute. I love how you always pretend that if my family doesn't like you, it must be because they're prejudiced. Never just because you're a total slimeball.

BEN: You don't really mean that.

(She moves away from him, toward the crib)

JOANIE: Look, I don't know how you got in here—or what you think you're doing—but I want you out. Right now! Because if you've come here to make trouble—

BEN: *(Goes to her)* Joanie, I *love* you! And you still love me too!

JOANIE: *(Surprised)* What are you talking about?

BEN: I *know* you do! I heard you with your father!

JOANIE: No—you're wrong—let go of me! *(She pulls away from him, moves down left toward the small table. He follows)*

BEN: Just let me finish! *(Pause; proudly)* Joanie . . . I've stopped smoking!

(She stares at him, exasperated)

Okay, I mean, I know that's not such a big thing, but I don't *lie* to myself about it anymore. And those, you know, those *attacks* I always got?—where I thought it was my heart?—I *never* get those now.

JOANIE: Ben, this is crazy! *(She crosses to the french doors, determined to escape, but he catches her, spins her gently back downstage)*

BEN: Maybe so! Maybe it is! But maybe it's *time* for a little craziness! Joanie, I *do* stuff now! I make appointments, I cook, clean up—don't you see? Living alone, I've *had* to do that stuff, or it wouldn't get done! What am I saying? Make *sense!* Make *sense!* Joanie—what I'm trying to say is—I've *changed.* Can't you see that?

JOANIE: *(Pause)* I don't understand. Are you saying that because you've gotten better at living alone, we should live together again?

BEN: Joanie, I'm *saying* it would all be different this time, I *swear* it would! *(He sees the rocker, edges her over to it and seats her there tenderly)* I want to *do* things for you—look —I want to take care of you! You *need* me!

JOANIE: Ben, I can't just—this is all too fast—

BEN: Joanie, look what's happening to you! Just take a look around this room for a minute! *(Pacing)* This isn't you! It isn't me! This is your *parents'* taste. Is that what you want to become? Joanie, you should be *yourself* again—you should be painting—you should have your rainbow back!

JOANIE: How dare you even *mention* my—

BEN: It's not just us, Joanie! It's *bigger* than just us now. We've got little Danny to think about too. From the first moment I saw him—from that very first moment in the hospital—

JOANIE: You said he looked boiled!

BEN: *(Slight pause)* Yeah, well—he *doesn't* anymore! Joanie, when I saw him again today—when I looked into those incredible little eyes—I said to myself, "What the hell are we *doing* here? Doesn't he deserve for us to try just a little bit harder? Doesn't he deserve to grow up with *two* parents, instead of one?"

JOANIE: *(Hesitates)* You really mean that?

BEN: I want to be a daddy to him, Joanie! A little guy like that *needs* a daddy. I want to play with him, I want to teach him stuff. I want to—to take him fishing!

JOANIE: You always hated fishing.

BEN: Oh, Joanie, I want to bait his hook and not even be grossed out by the worm! Don't you understand? Life! *(He moves about the room, passionate, animated)* I'm tired of running *away* from *life!* I want to just *do* stuff, and worry about it later. I want to *embrace* life! *All* of it—even the worms! Because that's what life is, Joanie—life is worms and stuff too! And I want to *share* those worms with you and little Danny! Not the worms. Forget the worms! But all three of us *together* again, just the way it should be! The way it *always* should've been, right from the start! Joanie, I know I've screwed up—I've made terrible mistakes—but it's not too late to make it right again. Life, Joanie, *life!* God! *Life!*

JOANIE: *(Pause; trembling)* Ben, I—I want to believe you, but—

(He goes to her, pulls her up from the chair, backing toward center)

BEN: Joanie, that selfish asshole that you walked out on, all those weeks ago—that asshole wouldn't even *be* here now. Can't you see I've changed . . . ? *(She hesitates, still torn)* I'm begging you now for another chance. Let me help you . . . Let me take care of you . . . Joanie, I *love you!*

JOANIE: *(A long wail)* Oh, Ben—it's been so *horrible . . . !* *(She bursts into tears and throws her arms around him)*

BEN: Oh, *yes! (They embrace hungrily; he spins her around, lifting her off the floor. Then he comforts her as she tries to talk between spasms of crying)*

JOANIE: They think I'm crazy . . . !

BEN: There, there—it's okay now—

JOANIE: Ben, my own *parents* seriously think I'm crazy!

BEN: So what? They've *always* thought I was crazy.

JOANIE: But you don't understand—I'm scared they might be right!

BEN: Then, we'll both be crazy together! *(Kissing her forehead)* Crazy in love!

JOANIE: *(Feverish)* No—no, Ben, *listen* to me! *(She breaks free from him, going to sit on the edge of the chaise)* You remember those games we used to play—all those awful problems we made up that we might have to face someday as parents?

(He grins, crossing to kneel in front of her)

BEN: Sure, I remember: "Tough Questions."

JOANIE: Ben, they're *all true!*

BEN: Oh, c'mon, honey . . . it can't be *that* bad—

JOANIE: It's worse! *Worse* than we ever *dreamed* it could be!

BEN: *(Slight pause)* It is?

89

JOANIE: *(Hugs him)* Oh not all of it, Ben—I'm not saying *all* of it is bad. There are some nice moments, there really are . . . But ninety-five percent of it is just *awful!*

BEN: Ninety-five?

JOANIE: Ben, it's a nightmare! You try to act like you know what you're doing, just to keep your spirits up, but half the time you have no *idea! (A bitter laugh)* One book says let him cry, he needs the exercise, but then the next book says no, pick him up or he'll feel helpless—and then which*ever* one I do, my mother says I'm spoiling him! *(She rises, moving around excitedly. He remains kneeling by the chaise)* Oh, Ben, after a while you just feel like some kind of *zombie!* You feed, jiggle, and wipe. All day, all night—that's all you do! Feed, jiggle, and wipe! You don't have a single minute to call your own, except when you're sleeping, but you can forget about *that,* 'cause you're never going to sleep again anyway! *(She laughs giddily)* Oh, but what difference does it make? *(She rushes to him, kneels to hug him)* You're here, Ben—here to share the load with me! Forever and ever and ever!

BEN: *(Manfully)* That's right, sweetheart. Forever!

(She rises again, energized and happy)

JOANIE: Oh God, honey, you won't even *believe* what it's like! It's like—like being on some weird roller-coaster ride, only it never stops, and you can never get off again! And every once in a while this big hand reaches down from the sky and says, "Okay, you handled *that* one pretty well, now let's see how you deal with . . . *this!* And then WHOMP! —it throws a switch or something and all of a sudden there's some sickening curve that you never even thought of! Oh, but you're *here* now—you'll be *with* me! *(He rises as she crosses to clutch him again)* That's all that matters, Ben —that you finally want to take care of me!

90

BEN: Honey, of *course* I do!

JOANIE: *You'll* do all the awful stuff that I just can't deal with! Like—like this morning! Oh God! *(She goes to the dresser, demonstrating. He crosses a bit weakly toward the crib, grasping it for support)* I was trying to get him dressed for church and we were running late, so of *course* he started peeing in my face. Well, that's not unusual—he pees in my face all the time. But after a while you just sort of get used to it . . . oh, you'll see! *(She hurries to him impulsively, kisses his cheek, then returns to the dresser)* But anyway this *morning,* before I could even, you know, block the stream of pee, he started having diarrhea at the same time! And then I did something really dumb, I jerked him up in the air too fast, and Ben—*that's* when it happened!

BEN: *(Horrified)* There's more?

JOANIE: He threw up on me too! *(Laughing, an edge of hysteria)* Ben, you never saw anything like it in your life! It was coming out of *every hole at once!* I mean, which one do you wipe *first?* (BEN *shrugs, trying to laugh, as if this were the most amusing puzzler he'd ever heard.* JOANIE *stumbles toward the chaise, weak from giggling)* And of course he's squirming like a cat the whole time and screaming bloody murder—well, I just panicked! I just totally panicked and burst into tears! But don't you *see?* *(He stares at her, uncomprehending) Now* when that happens, there'll be two of us! You can hold him down while I wipe! Or else *I* could hold him down while *you* wipe!

BEN: Sure. Whichever . . .

JOANIE: Oh, Ben, I'm so glad you're *here* now . . . ! *(She sags back onto the pile of coats with a deep sigh of relief. Then suddenly she sits bolt upright, struck by a wonderful new thought)* Sweetheart? I've got an idea! *(She runs to him, takes his hand)* Let's go tell Mom and Dad! *(She starts*

*for the french doors, but his unbudging weight pulls her
back. He looks at her, aghast)*

BEN: Right now?

JOANIE: *(Straightening his tie)* Oh, honey, they've been so
ashamed about the divorce—and so worried about me—I
just know it's spoiled this whole party for them. Let's do it!
Let's make this a *real* celebration. *(Sees his hesitation)* Ben,
they'll be so happy to hear we're back together!

BEN: Honey, I *know*, but I mean, this is like a major *thing*
here. We can't just . . . I mean, think what a *shock* this
would be to their systems, huh . . . ? *(He pats her shoulders, then moves away, toward the chaise)* And all those
other people in there, your *relatives?* We can't just . . . I
mean, shouldn't we maybe *talk* about this or something?

JOANIE: *(Pause)* You're chicken.

BEN: No! Of course not! I just think maybe we should *talk*
about this.

JOANIE: I thought you wanted to just *do* stuff, and worry
about it later.

BEN: Honey, I *do*, I do just want to do stuff . . .

JOANIE: Don't call me honey. I thought you said you'd
changed, Ben.

BEN: I *have* changed!

JOANIE: What happened to the guy who was tired of running
away all the time? What happened to "Life, Life, Life!"

BEN: Honey, *I've* changed, but your parents haven't! They'd
rip me limb from limb!

92

JOANIE: You *weasel*. You haven't changed one *bit*. You're still just the same baby you always were! And I let myself think *you* could take care of *me* . . . what an idiot I was!

BEN: Aw, Joanie, *c'mon* now—that's not fair! I love you!

JOANIE: Baby! *(Suddenly shouting)* GREAT—BIG—OVER-GROWN—*BABY!*

(BEN *is alarmed at her volume. He waves his hands frantically)*

BEN: Joanie, don't—Ssshhhh!—they'll hear you!

JOANIE: *(Still shouting)* That's all you are! YOU'RE JUST ANOTHER BABY! *(She goes suddenly to the french doors. He rises, starts for her)*

BEN: Honey, what—what're you—NO!—DON'T DO THAT! *(She struggles past him and flings the doors wide open. She goes into the hallway, shouting, while he tries to pull her back by one arm)*

JOANIE: HEY, EVERYBODY—COME HERE! COME SEE THE GIANT BABY! *(She comes back in, crossing toward the kitchen. He falls to his knees, pleading)*

BEN: Joanie, no—Joanie, for God's sake!—

JOANIE: COME ONE, COME ALL! STEP RIGHT THIS WAY!

BEN: Oh, God! Oh, God . . . !

JOANIE: *(Through the kitchen door)* SEE the *incredible* MAN-SIZED INFANT! He WALKS! He TALKS! He HUGS! He KISSES! He TELLS LIES . . . !

(BEN *jumps up, looking for some way out of this disaster. He sees the pile of coats on the chaise, races to them, grabs up the top coat and puts it on, turning up the collar in a mad attempt at disguise. The coat is much too big for him. He grabs a tweed hat as well, tugs it down over his head, then scurries up into the hallway, hoping to bluff his way through the party. He disappears momentarily, then we hear confused shouting from the living room, and he runs back into the nursery. All the while,* JOANIE *continues to pace about on her rampage*)

SEE the MAN-CHILD! Incredible but TRUE! Thirty-five years of AGE, friends, and yet TOTALLY UNABLE to ACCEPT RESPONSIBILITY . . . !

(BEN *grabs up a couple more overcoats, holding them over his head, then sits on the floor, rolling himself into a ball. He drapes the coats to cover his legs and feet, and within seconds is completely hidden. He holds perfectly still.* JOANIE *sees what he's up to, but keeps raving on*)

Oh yes, friends, He LOOKS like a GROWN-UP, but DON'T BE FOOLED! He's the INCREDIBLE GIANT BABY . . . !

(*She goes up into the hallway, disappears for a moment, then reappears, tugging along in her wake three or four of the party guests*) Come ONE, come ALL! Admission is FREE! THE SHOW IS JUST BEGINNING . . . !

(*Aunt Bonnie is there, and perhaps Cousin Ruth. Certainly Reverend Weeboldt. They all crowd into the doorway, drinks in hand, watching in amazement.* CHARLOTTE *pushes her way through them, and* GIL *appears at this same moment through the kitchen door*)

CHARLOTTE: Oh, my *Lord* . . . !

JOANIE: You want to be a BABY? You want to be a BABY for the rest of your life? FINE! But you're gonna need THE RIGHT EQUIPMENT!

CHARLOTTE: *(Under her breath)* She's *talking* to a pile of *coats*, Gilbert . . .

GIL: I can *see* that, dear!

(JOANIE races to the dresser, pulls open a drawer, grabs at the contents)

JOANIE: How 'bout some *nappies*, Ben? You'll need plenty of nappies! *(She hurls diapers at him, one after another, then grabs for other items)*

GIL: *Ben . . . ?*

JOANIE: Oh, and how about a *rattle?* Teething ring! Pacifier! That's a good one for you, Ben, you'll *love* that one!

CHARLOTTE: *(To the guests, desperately)* It's—It's a *game* we play! It's make-believe!

(JOANIE runs to the crib, pulls out the stuffed duck, throws it at BEN)

JOANIE: DUCK! *(She runs to the pile of gifts on the small table)*

CHARLOTTE: *(Trying to laugh)* Sometimes he's in the coats, and other times he's in the furniture! Where are you *this* time, you silly old Ben . . . ?

JOANIE: *(Throwing gifts)* Spoon! Spoon! Spoon! Spoon! *(She circles back toward the dresser for more ammunition. The guests watch, mystified, as CHARLOTTE moves gaily about the room, talking to the floors, walls, etc.)*

CHARLOTTE: Are you in there? Ooooo! We know you're in here *somewhere*, Ben! *(Stamps her feet)* Come out, come out, wherever you are! Allee-allee-all-in-free!

GIL: Charlotte, for God's sake!

JOANIE: How about some *cotton balls*, Ben? Better than no balls at all! *(She jumps up onto the chaise and shakes a box of cotton balls down onto him. When it's empty, she will jump down and go back to the dresser. She will pull out* BEN*'s wine bottle, start to throw it, then realize she doesn't know what it's doing there. She will look back in the drawer, confused)*

CHARLOTTE: *(On* JOANIE*'s initial action)* Oh, ah—yes!—are we in the *coats* today? *Sneaky* old Ben! Are we playing hidey-widey in the coatsy-woats? *(She picks up a coat sleeve and tugs on it playfully. Immediately it is jerked in the other direction. Startled, she gives it another pull, and this time it's yanked all the way out of her hand. She shrieks and backs off.* GIL *rushes over and pulls off the coats, revealing* BEN. CHARLOTTE *and* GIL *gasp.* BEN *smiles up at* GIL *weakly)*

BEN: Mr. Hockaday! Lookin' good!

(With an angry roar, GIL *tosses the coats aside, then leaps at* BEN, *trying to strangle him.* BEN *tries to crawl away, but* GIL *catches him, upstage of the chaise, and pins him there, pummeling him. The "landing" of any blows is obscured by the chaise. Ad-lib threats from* GIL, *pleas from* BEN—*or perhaps it's mainly a matter of snarls and growls. It's all very one-sided—*BEN *has no wish to hurt* GIL—*and not really very dangerous—*GIL *gets quickly winded, and in fact by the end of it is pounding* BEN *with the stuffed duck. At any rate, their noisy battle continues during the following.* JOANIE, *at the dresser, has by now also found* BEN*'s prayer book and yarmulka. She sets aside the wine bottle, then crosses over to*

*the rocker—calmly ignoring the chaos on all sides—to sit
and examine her discoveries. The guests stand rooted in
shock and fascination.* CHARLOTTE, *trying as best she can to
compose herself, confronts them with her most dazzling
smile)*

CHARLOTTE: We're having a little family discussion just now
. . . I wonder if you'd mind terribly going back into the
living room? There's a lovely quiche that's hardly been
touched . . .

(She pushes them firmly out into the hallway)

Thank you . . . thank you *so* much . . . Just, you know,
separate into small groups and chat amongst yourselves.
Yes, 'bye now! . . . Yes, lovely, thank you . . .

*(One last guest, more reluctant than the others to go, requires
an almost brutal shove)*

Thank you, damn it!

*(She shuts the french doors, then hurries to separate the two
struggling men. She seizes* GIL'*s arm)*

Gilbert, *stop this!* Stop this immediately! You'll hurt yourself!

GIL: Let me at the bastard!

CHARLOTTE: He's not worth it, Gil! . . . Let him go . . .

GIL: I'll rip his lungs out!

CHARLOTTE: *Please* stop it! *(She finally manages to pull* GIL
free, and to his feet. He sways dizzily) Are you all right,
darling? He didn't bite you, did he? He didn't break the
skin?

97

GIL: He nev . . . He nev . . .

CHARLOTTE: There, there, now—

GIL: Never laid a . . . glove on me . . .

(CHARLOTTE *eases him over to the chaise, where he collapses on his back. She loosens his tie, unbuttons his collar.* BEN *is crawling toward the crib, dazed*)

CHARLOTTE: Just try to get your wind back. *(To* BEN*)* You must be *so* pleased. Your little scheme worked *wonderfully*.

BEN: What *scheme!?*

CHARLOTTE: You deliberately set out to humiliate us! To ruin this party and upset our guests! You've probably killed my husband into the bargain.

(BEN *pulls himself to his feet, using the crib for support*)

BEN: Lady, I never wanted to see your face again. Bet on it.

CHARLOTTE: You're a destroyer, Ben. You destroy everything and everyone you touch . . .

(*She helps* GIL *to sit upright. He puts his face in his hands, still a bit winded*)

Well, you won't destroy our little girl. Thank God she's out of your grasp now! And you won't destroy our grandson, either. *You* bet on *that.*

(BEN *takes off the hat and overcoat, throwing them aside*)

BEN: I *love* Joanie! And I love Daniel!

CHARLOTTE: You don't love anyone but yourself. You never will.

BEN: What the hell do *you* know about love? I climbed on top of *garbage* cans out there . . . I crawled up six flights of rusty ladders . . . I've been cut, bruised, cramped, soaked, clobbered, and . . . and *cotton-balled!* I'm a goddamn *fugitive* at my own son's *christening!*

CHARLOTTE: He's not your son anymore! He no longer concerns you! From now on we'll decide what's best for Daniel.

BEN: Hey, I may still be confused about a few things—I *may* even have screwed up my entire *life*—but you let me decide what *concerns* me, okay? He's *my* son, not yours! And I'm not gonna just stand around and watch while you turn him into some kind of . . . of . . . *golfer! (He turns away from them angrily.* GIL *looks up at him, impressed in spite of himself by this passion.* CHARLOTTE *is very angry, but before she can respond,* JOANIE *interrupts, rising from her chair)*

JOANIE: Ben, why did you bring this beanie?

BEN: What beanie?

JOANIE: The prayer book, the wine . . . the yarmulka. *(She holds it up)* Why?

(BEN *turns, sees what she's talking about. He is abruptly self-conscious. He goes to her and snatches back the book and yarmulka)*

BEN: Never mind that . . . *(He crosses to the dresser, gets out his backpack, and stuffs in the wine bottle and prayer book)*

JOANIE: Ben, you haven't set foot in a synagogue since your bar mitzvah!

BEN: C'mon, huh?

JOANIE: The only thing Jewish about you is that you know all the jokes!

BEN: Gimme a break! *(Pause)* I said a few prayers, that's all . . . I didn't have a *minyan* or a *mohel* or any of that other good stuff, so it probably won't even count . . . Aw, what's the use, Joanie? Look at them!

CHARLOTTE: We've got nothing against your religion, Ben. It's *you* we hate.

GIL: Let him finish, Charlotte.

CHARLOTTE: *(Startled)* Why are you taking *his* part?

GIL: All I said was let him finish!

BEN: It's his *naming* day. What the hell else was I going to give him . . . ?

(Pause. He looks at the yarmulka, twisting it in his hands. To all three of them)

This is *part* of me, whether I like it or not. It's part of him, too, now . . . We *share* this. And we always will, no matter how many times we both screw it up . . . We can make jokes about it, we can try to ignore it—but those are still just ways of admitting that it matters. *(Pause)* It matters, Joanie . . . *(Pause)* So go ahead and laugh at me.

(He stuffs the yarmulka into the backpack, buckles it closed)

My own parents will hardly even speak to me anymore, did you know that . . . ? It's true. I'm a lousy Jew, I always have been.

CHARLOTTE: You're a lousy human being.

(BEN *angrily tosses the backpack down on the rocker*)

BEN: Oh, why don't you just give it a rest!

GIL: Hey! You show some respect!

BEN: Why should I? She never showed any to me!

CHARLOTTE: You're no good for her! Why can't you just admit it?

BEN: Oh, look who's talking!

GIL: You're breaking my little girl's heart!

(*They all begin shouting at once—ad-lib accusations and challenges.* JOANIE *gets between* BEN *and her parents*)

JOANIE: *Stop it!* All of you just *stop* it! (*Pause. They look at her. She points quickly to each*) *You're* wrong! *You're* wrong! *You're* wrong! You're right—you're right—you're right! What *difference* does it make? (*Pause. To* BEN) They're not the bad guys here, okay? So just—get off their case. (*To her parents*) And he's not the bad guy either.

GIL: Ha!

JOANIE: I know you don't believe that, but it's true. (*Pause*) Mom—Dad—I know you only want what's best for me and Danny. But you're also trying to tell me what that is! Can't you see? I just—I can't be your "little girl" anymore. That doesn't mean I don't love you, 'cause I do. But I need you to

101

let that go now. *(Pause)* Ben . . . oh, God, Ben. I always wanted to somehow . . . paint a rainbow over us. I just needed to see it so much, sometimes I couldn't see anything else. And that was *wrong*, Ben. You were right to be mad about it. But that's *over*, it doesn't matter anymore . . . I can't spend the rest of my life just taking care of you! I'm a mother now. And for that to work—it's going to take all the best stuff that's in me. *(Pause)* Mom, could I have the key to the window lock?

CHARLOTTE: What for?

JOANIE: It's for Ben. *(Pause)* Please, Mom . . .

(CHARLOTTE *takes it from her pocket, hands it over reluctantly*)

Thank you. Now would you both go out and get the baby for me?

CHARLOTTE: *(Surprised)* The baby? Oh, Joanie—no! He'll take him—he'll kidnap him out the window!

JOANIE: *(Gently)* No. He won't do that.

GIL: Are you sure you know what you're doing, honey?

JOANIE: Dad, I hope so.

(They hesitate a moment longer, looking at her, then something in her face convinces them. They exit reluctantly through the french doors, leaving them open. JOANIE turns, smiles to BEN. A pause. This is all taking so much more courage than she really feels)

I keep saying to myself, I won't think about next month, or next year—or even tomorrow. Those words don't mean anything. Right now I'll just try to help him stop crying.

'Cause if I can only help him to stop crying, then I might make it till dawn. And if I make it till dawn, who knows? *(She smiles)* I might even make it till lunchtime.

(She goes to the window, unlocks the padlock, removes it. A brief pause)

That's how it works, Ben. You just keep taking one little step at a time, trying to . . . make friends with chaos. That may not sound like much, but believe me—it's a lot.

(She sets the padlock down on the sill, swings open the gate, then steps aside)

If you want to go—*(She tries for a breezy manner)*—then hey!—looky here—you won't even have to see me again. *(Then, all at once, fighting tears)* I love you, Ben. I always will. And there's nothing I want more than for us to somehow work this out. But Ben, if you can't help me—then I need for you to not be another one of my problems. *(Pause)* And most of all, sweetheart, I need for you to decide about it, right now.

BEN: *(Pause; very quietly)* I'm scared, Joanie.

JOANIE: I am too, baby.

BEN: Not of Danny. *(Pause)* What if I can't love him enough?

JOANIE: *(Gently)* What if you never try?

(GIL reenters, rolling the bassinet. He pushes it down to a position, center, between BEN and JOANIE. Then he retreats back to one side of the doorway, where CHARLOTTE stands watching. He puts his arm around her. JOANIE goes to the bassinet, reaches in to stroke the baby's face. She looks up)

Look for yourself, Ben. Look and decide.

(She starts to go, then impulsively returns. She gives BEN *a quick kiss on the cheek. She is still fighting tears)*

It all starts with just one step.

(She turns quickly and hurries off through the french doors, passing her parents. CHARLOTTE *and* GIL *stare at* BEN. *A pause.* CHARLOTTE *looks as if she might be about to say something, but stops herself.* GIL *looks at her, awaiting some signal. She turns and exits stiffly through the french doors, without a backward glance.* GIL *follows her off quietly, leaving* BEN *alone.* BEN *hesitates only a moment before going to the rocker and grabbing his backpack. He crosses quickly to the window, averting his eyes from the bassinet as he passes it. He pushes the window up, in one determined motion, then starts to climb out onto the fire escape. He hesitates, stops. He leans his forehead against the glass, staring out. Freedom is so very close. He looks back at the bassinet for a moment, then lowers his backpack to the floor)*

BEN: Look, maybe . . . maybe I'll just say good-bye to you. But that's *all*.

(Slowly, reluctantly, he crosses over to the bassinet and looks down. The lights have begun to slowly dim, except at center, around BEN *and the bassinet)*

I never picked you up before, so maybe I'll do that, too. But it doesn't *mean* anything, pal, so don't get any big ideas . . .

(He reaches down to pick up the baby but hesitates, uncertain quite how his hands should go. He looks longingly toward the french doors, but no one is going to help him with this. He takes a deep breath and then carefully picks up the baby, cradling him uncertainly against his shoulder. The baby wears a long, beautiful white lace christening gown)

Okay, there . . . I picked you up. Big fucking deal!

(Not knowing what else to do, he gives the baby one or two tentative little pats. He shakes his head with self-conscious derision)

"Father!"

(Pause. With wonder at the sound)

Father . . .

(Pause. For the first and only time in this act, he looks out and sees the audience. With a note of rising panic)

Now what?!

(BLACKOUT & CURTAIN)

END OF PLAY

PRODUCTION NOTES

Though *Little Footsteps* can certainly be performed without any incidental music, the use of such a score, composed by John McKinney, greatly enhanced the original New York production. His music was used to introduce each act, to underscore the two Act I fantasy scenes (pp. 5–7 and pp. 24–27), as well as the last scene of Act II (pp. 103–105) and to punctuate the final curtain. A tape of Mr. McKinney's music for *Little Footsteps* is available for rental and may be obtained by contacting DRAMATISTS PLAY SERVICE, INC., 440 Park Avenue South, New York, NY 10016.

The original setting for the play, as designed by Thomas Lynch, was quite small—small enough that an actor could cross virtually the entire playing area, left to right, on a single line of dialogue. This was a deliberate artistic choice, rather than a practical necessity, and certainly the play could be performed successfully on a larger set. But because the stage directions in this edition reflect blocking done for that small set (and very clever blocking, indeed, devised by director Gary Pearle), they should be taken as general indicators of the sort of action and timing that I envision, rather than as strict requirements.

107

The paints used by Ben and Joanie (mostly Joanie) in Act I should be washable poster paints—the colors are bold and bright, the "look" is suitably childlike, and any stray splatters can be easily cleaned from hands, costumes, etc. The trick for Joanie, who does the actual work, is to paint mostly on Ben's dialogue and face out on her own; she can thereby avoid upstaging herself.

The set changeover was accomplished by making the Act II (nursery) walls "permanent." The Act I walls, divided into sectional panels for ease of operation, were superimposed over the Act II walls, sliding into grooves formed by the moldings around the floor, ceiling, window, and doors; the moldings, therefore, were actually holding the Act I walls in place (along with concealed clips at their downstage, or "wing," edges). At the end of Act I, the curtain would fall, and stagehands would slide the newly painted wall panels out of their grooves, revealing the Act II walls beneath. We rotated half a dozen different sets of Act I wall panels, since some were always in use (two sets on matinee days), while others were waiting to be repainted and restenciled. (Joanie's painting of the Act I walls—and Ben's vandalization of them —were actually choreographed so that not every panel had to be repainted after every performance, but only a certain few.) The set changeover, even with all the "dressing" of props and furniture required for the nursery, took less than ten minutes.

The party guests who briefly (and wordlessly) appear on pp. 94–97 were, by special permission of Actor's Equity, members of the backstage crew, suitably dressed for the christening. Later, when the show's run extended beyond its initial contract, these walk-ons were played by the Equity understudies, which seems to me the most businesslike arrangement for other professional theatres to follow. In amateur theatres, of course, these guests might be played by any available stagestruck friends of the company.

I think the play is reasonably free from confusing and/or strictly regional references. "Clio Awards" (p. 21) are the advertising world's equivalent of Oscars. "Leona Helmsley" (p. 35), a New York City hotel hostess and owner, has a (locally) famous flair for self-promotion (equivalent names for Ben's joke might include Pia Zadora, Imelda Marcos, or Judge Wapner.) Ben's Hebrew words, since they're spelled out phonetically in English, shouldn't present much trouble —with the possible exception of *"mohel"* (p. 100), which is pronounced "moil."

The "baby" which starts crying after Ben touches its lips with wine (p. 71), is of course played by a tape recorder concealed in the bassinet; Ben's action here allows him to operate the machine himself. However, the baby which Gil rolls onstage in the bassinet for the play's final scene (p. 103), and which Ben subsequently picks up, should at all costs be a *real baby*. This obviously presents many problems, which I hate to wish on subsequent productions of the play, but I think the moment demands it; any other solution would be anticlimactic. After all, the paint is real in Act I, and the finger sandwiches are real in Act II; should Ben's son, when it comes to the moment he is finally revealed, be any less real? Or, to put it another way, what does it signify if Ben finally comes to some degree of emotional acceptance of his own parenthood, only to show us that his offspring is a plastic doll?

After some initial debate about whether live babies come under the heading of "casting" or "props" (casting lost the argument, and then had to, in the very capable hands of Amy Introcaso, make the search), we located our infants by contacting maternity centers, by posting notices in nearby apartment buildings, and by word of mouth. In the end we rotated four babies (all boys, though they needn't have been), allowing for the rigors of an eight-performance week, as well as the fact that babies tend to get the sniffles from time to time, and are notoriously lax about schedules. The parents were paid a small stipend, and the usual practice was for the baby's mother to bring him to the theatre during the second act, feed him backstage (or whatever ritual seemed most calming), oversee his placement in the prop bassinet, and then wait in the wings to receive him after the first curtain call (for safety reasons, the actor playing Ben stayed in position following the final blackout, and the first bow, a company bow, included the live baby). All told, only about a half hour of the baby's (and his mother's) time was required for each show. The babies ranged in age from three months to about seven (it would have been impractical, perhaps even illegal, to use the month-old baby spoken of in the script), their size being disguised somewhat by the christening gown.

A prop doll baby, dressed in a second christening gown, was always kept ready backstage, in case the live baby was fussing too much to go on. This determination could be made almost up to the last second by the stage managers. However, the substitution very rarely occurred, as our babies tended to be remarkably mellow performers (calmness ranked even above cuteness as a criterion for their selection). If the baby whimpered or gurgled quietly during his time onstage, that of course was fine—it even enhanced Ben's helplessness in the moment, his need to pick up and comfort his son. In one dreadful performance, though, the inevitable came to pass—a baby began shrieking so loudly, so inconsolably, that Ben could not be heard, nor could he take his customary timing in terms of actions, and the ending was rather spoiled. To arm us against another such occurrence, I devised an alternate, "emergency" ending, and thereafter we all felt much safer as the final moments of the play approached. This alternate ending follows as an appendix.

To maintain the element of surprise, we listed neither the party guests nor the babies in the program; instead they received lobby billing following each performance. We also squelched any mention of the live babies in our advertising, publicity articles, and so forth. And it worked: the babies added real magic to the final moments of the play, and even the critics were charmed into keeping our little secret.

I cannot conclude without expressing my great appreciation to Andre Bishop, the artistic director of Playwrights

Horizons, who commissioned and then produced this play, and to Gary Pearle, who shepherded the script through so many discussions and revisions and then directed it so lovingly and well. This play could not have been born without them.

—Ted Tally

April 14, 1986
New York City

APPENDIX
ALTERNATE ENDING IF BABY CRIES

(GIL *reenters, pushing the bassinet. The baby is crying. He pushes it down center, then retreats back to* CHARLOTTE's *side.* JOANIE *goes to the bassinet*)

JOANIE: Look for yourself, Ben. Look and decide. *(She goes straight to him, kisses him)* It all starts with just one step.

(She turns quickly, hurries off through the french doors. CHARLOTTE *and* GIL *hesitate only a moment, looking at* BEN, *then exit.* BEN *goes quickly to the window, but the crying stops him. He turns, looks at the bassinet for a moment. He's alone, there's no one else to comfort the baby. He crosses to it)*

NOTE: ACTOR'S DECISION *NOT* TO RAISE THE WINDOW CUES THE STAGE MANAGER THAT HE HAS CHOSEN THE SHORTER ENDING. S.M. WARNS ALL FINAL LIGHT AND SOUND CUES FOR A FASTER "GO."

BEN: *(At bassinet)* Hey, don't cry . . . Don't cry, Danny . . . Look, maybe I'll pick you up, okay? But just till you stop crying, and that's *it!*

(He picks the baby up, cradles it against his shoulder, and does his best to soothe it. He might try rocking it, or kissing it,

113

or whispering. This moment of attempted comforting should not be rushed. But when all else fails, he looks out at the audience. A beat. Then, with genuine panic)

Now what?!

(BLACKOUT. END OF PLAY)

ABOUT THE AUTHOR

Ted Tally was born in North Carolina in 1952 and educated at Yale College and the Yale School of Drama. His plays, which include *Terra Nova, Hooters, Coming Attractions,* and *Silver Linings,* have premiered Off-Broadway and have also been produced at regional theatres throughout the United States. In addition, he has written for film and television. His honors include the Outer Critics Circle Award for best new American play, an Obie Award, a Dramalogue Award, and playwriting fellowships from the National Endowment for the Arts and the Guggenheim Foundation.